Vintage & Historic RACING·CARS

by Alex Gabbard

Edited by Dean Batchelor

ACKNOWLEDGMENTS

The author wishes to extend great appreciation to the following people who have contributed to making this book possible:

A special thanks to Fred Puhn whose direction and contributions led to this book becoming a reality.

Ron Sessions, Tom Monroe and the staff of HPBooks who have made this superb book what it is.

Another special thanks to Dean Batchelor whose guidance and interest is greatly appreciated.

Ford and Kate Heacock, Roger Cope and the staff of the Sportscar Vintage Racing Association and to the members of SVRA whose cars have become the body this book.

Steve Simpson, Howard Turner, John Steen, staff and members of the Walter Mitty Challenge.

Steve Earle and staff of the Historic Motor Sport Association and its member cars illustrated in this book.

John Burgess and staff of the Briggs Cunningham Automotive Museum 250 E. Baker St. Costa Mesa, CA 92626

The staff of the Pebble Beach Company and the Pebble Beach Concours.

A special thanks to John and Toddie Wyer, Brian Redman, John Cooper, Jim Hall, Carroll Shelby, Bob Bondurant and Roy Salvadori who gave me a lot of their time for the personal interviews expressed in this book, and especially for the privilege of getting to know them. They are some of the wonderful people who lived a great portion of the history recorded in this book.

Otis Meyer, *Road & Track* Magazine
Bob D'Olivo, Petersen Publishing Co.
Art Eastman, Photographer
Mary Gabbard, Squire Gabbard, Wesley Gabbard, In-House Photographers

And many thanks to all the owners and drivers who have given me the opportunity to learn about their superb cars and to photograph them for this book. It has been great fun!

2

ANOTHER FACT-FILLED AUTOMOTIVE BOOK FROM HPBooks®

Publisher: Rick Bailey; Executive Editor: Randy Summerlin;
Editorial Director: Tom Monroe, P.E., S.A.E.;
Senior Editor: Ron Sessions, A.S.A.E.;
Art Director: Don Burton; Book Design: Paul Fitzgerald;
Production Coordinator: Cindy J. Coatsworth; Typography: Michelle Carter;
Director of Manufacturing: Anthony B. Narducci;
Front Cover Photos: Alex Gabbard
Back Cover Photos: Alex Gabbard and Petersen Publishing Co.

Published by HPBooks
a Division of HPBooks, Inc.
P.O. Box 5367, Tucson, AZ 85703 602/888-2150
ISBN 0-89586-405-3 Library of Congress Catalog Number 86-81203
© 1986 HPBooks, Inc. Printed in Singapore
1st Printing

CONTENTS

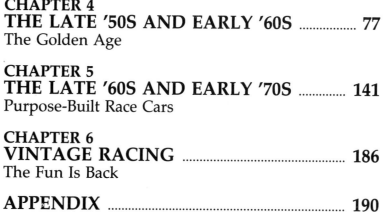

3

This book is dedicated to Mary who has lived
a love affair with cars with me

and to Squire and Wesley who have grown up with the
sports cars I grew up with

and to the memory of all the people who have
contributed to the great legacy that is
sports cars and racing.

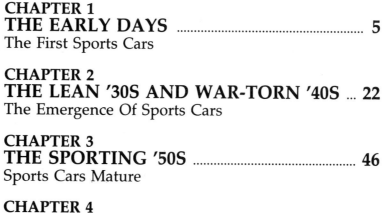

FOREWORD

This interesting and informative book will be of considerable value not only to those who remember these cars, but also to enthusiasts who enjoy reading about sports-car racing in days gone by. Many feel that the sights and sounds of magnificent cars, such as the Jaguar D Type, Ford GT-40, Cobra, Porsche 917, Lola T70, various Ferraris and the Swiss watch-like Bugattis, represent an era of motor racing that will never be repeated.

Alex Gabbard is to be congratulated on his concise and informative book.
Jacksonville, Florida, June 1986

Brian Redman

After spending most of my active life involved in motor racing and enjoying every minute of it, I think the nicest part has been the people I have met. Some play an active part and are there because they make their living that way; others because of a deep interest in and love of the sport that keeps bringing them back and making them an essential and welcome part of the overall scene.

Alex Gabbard is one of these. He is seriously interested in and very knowledgeable about motor racing and its history. By profession, he is a nuclear physicist, which I would have thought is sufficiently demanding for most people. It is a measure of his devotion to motor racing that he has been able to write this very good book. A professional historian would approach with trepidation a subject of such magnitude and scope. To catalog the history of the racing car almost from the earliest manifestations right down to the early 1970s is indeed a monumental task,

embracing as it does an almost incredible acceleration in development. Alex has achieved this formidable assignment with admirable clarity and continuity. It is a book to be read once for pleasure and then used as a permanent and valuable source of technical reference.

I recommend Alex's book for anyone interested in the history and development of the racing car. When speaking of the cars with which I am familiar, the book is accurate and factual and captures admirably the atmosphere of the time in which the action took place. I am sure it will give as much enjoyment to a great many people as it has to me.

Scottsdale, Arizona, June 1986

John Wyer

CHAPTER 1

THE EARLY DAYS

Henry Ford's famed racing car of 1903, the 999 is an example of very early-day automotive racing technology. Speeds of over 90 mph were achievable from 17.7 liters displacement. Road & Track photo.

As with horse racing, the first automobile race probably was the result of a difference of opinion: Whose car was the fastest? Early-day races usually ended with the last car running being the winner. In the 1890s, automobiles were still largely unreliable curiosities and certainly luxury items. However, races were held among builders to prove their products in public demonstrations. A Duryea, the second one built, won the first American automobile race held in 1895 near Chicago. The third Duryea built won an English race from London to Brighton the next year.

Although racing generated excitement anywhere there were cars, the French were the first to formally set up regulated competition. More than 20 cars took place in the first formal reliability run in 1894, a 79-mile event from Paris to Rouen. Sponsored by the French magazine, *Le Petit Journal*, such automotive events produced tremendous public interest which was the source for establishing the Automobile Club de France—ACF.

FORD 999
1903

17.7-liter/1080-CID in-line 4-cylinder
1600 lb, ash frame, no body
leaf-spring front suspension

In 1895, the ACF held the first long distance race between Paris and Bordeaux, a 732-mile enduro emphasizing speed and driver skill as well as reliability. It was won by a Panhard averaging 15 mph. Other inter-city races attracted hordes of spectators. The cars were surprisingly capable of perhaps 90 mph, and at those speeds along public roads lined with crowds of curious onlookers, races occasionally ended in tragedy.

In the Paris-to-Madrid race of 1903, two drivers, three mechanics and several spectators were killed in a series of accidents. Protests against racing resulted in improved safety for cars, drivers and spectators, an element that has remained an integral part of auto racing.

Each year, a variety of loosely organized competitive events were held. In 1903, newspaper magnate and owner of the *New York Herald*, James Gordon Bennett, founded the Gordon Bennett Cup series designed to foster technical development of cars through competition between national teams. Each country could enter three cars with the winner receiving wide international acclaim.

However, the series lasted only until 1906 when the restrictions of only three cars forming a team was surpassed by the ACF's introduction of *grand prix* racing. The ACF had become the dominant force in organized racing and rebelled against such tight restraints as set in the Gordon Bennett Cup races. The ACF held their first official race in 1906, the Grand Prix de L'Automobile de France, known as the French Grand Prix ever since, and set the pattern for modern grand prix racing. It was a 12-lap race around a 64-mile course near LeMans. From that beginning, Grand Prix racing has continued to attract private and factory teams that still generate arguments about whose cars are best, most reliable and fastest.

The Vanderbilt Cup races held on Long Island began in 1904 and served to formalize American racing. When the annual Indianapolis 500 was inaugurated in 1911, American racing became solidly founded.

BIG VERSUS LITTLE

Even in the early days of auto racing, two schools of thought prevailed: large, heavy cars fitted with big engines versus small, lightweight cars with small engines. An example of the first variety was Henry Ford's first hand-built racing car of 1901 in which he beat Alexander Winton. Winton was America's foremost driver at the time and builder of the famed Winton "Bullets."

Next came two more cars from Henry Ford, the Arrow and the 999, both built in 1903. At the time, the American land speed record was held by the New York Central locomotive, number 999, from which Ford took the name for his third racer. Both cars were rather crude and consisted of little more than a chassis and drive line with no bodywork. They weighed well over 1600 pounds each and used four-cylinder engines of 70 HP displacing 1080 cubic inches (17.7 liters). Ford achieved 91.37 mph aboard the Arrow on the ice of Lake St. Clair on January 12, 1904. That was the first time a car had exceeded 90 mph, but the record lasted for only two weeks. W. K. Vanderbilt, a wealthy aristocrat who later established the Vanderbilt Cup Races, purchased a Mercedes 90 and set a new record of 92.3 mph at Daytona Beach, Florida.

Contrasting the big-car/big-engine philosophy was the diminutive Packard Gray Wolf first raced in September, 1903. The Wolf was one of America's first lightweight racers and weighed only 1310 pounds. It was powered by a 275.6-CID (4.52-liter) in-line four-cylinder engine producing about 25 HP at 1000 rpm and was capable of more than 75 mph.

The Gray Wolf was designed by Charles Schmidt, a 34-year-old French engineer who had come to Packard from the Mors car company of France in the spring of 1902. At Mors, he was familiar with the company's 11.6-liter specials with streamlined front coachwork, but chose smaller cars when given the chance at Packard. Both Schmidt and Harry Cunningham, who had previously piloted the 999, drove the Wolf to

Compared to the norm for the time, the Packard Gray Wolf was an early example of lightweight design and small-displacement engine; an idea before its time. Don Fostle photo.

many successes in highly acclaimed races, some featuring the famed Barney Oldfield in 40- to 80-HP Wintons. Even with several failures and crashes during the 1903 season, the Wolf fared well and was used by Schmidt and Packard as a continually evolving experimental vehicle that tested several exhaust systems, carburetors and two-, three-, and four-speed transmissions among other ideas.

During the first Vanderbilt Cup race of October 8, 1904, the Wolf was by far the best known car. Eighteen cars started, but the race was called when enthusiastic spectators mobbed the track. Only seven cars were still running; one was Schmidt in the Gray Wolf. A huge 90-HP Panhard won the race, but in at 2nd was the Wolf. Following was another small car, a 24-HP Pope-Toledo. Oldfield noted the potential of moderately powered lightweight cars and proclaimed that his future cars would weigh no more than 1800 pounds. The Wolf's light weight and good aerodynamics helped it to set speed records for the kilometer, mile and 5-mile and posted times for the mile of 46.4 seconds at an average speed of 77.58 mph.

However, it was many years before the advantages of small, lightweight, well-balanced and efficient cars were widely appreciated.

Further examples of the "big" philosophy were the 12.5- and 15-liter Grand Prix Benz cars of 1908 that weighed over 2700 pounds, the 18-liter FIATs and 12.9-liter Renaults of 1906, the 17.2-liter DeDietrichs and most other cars of the day. The reason for staying big was due mostly to the available technology. Volumetric efficiency was low, so big cubes were needed to get the power. And big engines required big radiators, strong frames and heavy axles, thus weight was high.

Strangely, the general philosophy about braking during the first 30 years of motoring was that front brakes were *dangerous* and to be avoided. Because racing cars were built to go fast, little thought was given to stopping. Therefore, only feeble attempts were made to make brakes useful. In most cases, it took a driver's entire strength to operate a hand-lever-actuated friction clamp around axles or some other rotating shaft, then wait for the car to stop on its own. Driver control was a thing of the distant future.

PACKARD GRAY WOLF
1903

4.52-liter/275.6-CID in-line 4-cylinder
25 HP @ 1000 rpm
1310 lb, open aluminum body
transverse leaf-spring suspension

Driving such cars required men of strength and endurance, especially on durability runs like the 438-mile St. Petersburg-to-Moscow race of 1908. Roads were atrocious, but Frenchman Victor Hemery made the trek in 8 hours, 33 minutes and 48 seconds to win with his GP Benz at an average speed of 51.4 mph! To be battered around for hours in the completely open Benz required uncommon determination, and an admiring public elevated him to hero status.

Conditions were a little better in Grand Prix racing which was just beginning. The French GP of 1906 over a 64-mile circuit of closed public roads, planked cart paths and the like, was the site of a significant innovation. Heavy cars capable of rather remarkable speeds were rough on tires. John Boyd Dunlop had invented pneumatic tires, which served both the bicycle and automotive industries, but it was tire manufacturer Andre Michelin who solved the problem of lost time for tire changes.

Rules stated that only a driver and his mechanic could work on cars; no elaborate pit crews with truck loads of equipment in those days. A good team is said to have been able to replace a tire and tube in about 5 minutes. But, in racing, that is a lot of time lost, and a problem begging for a solution.

Michelin's idea was that tires and tubes be mounted on a rim. When a flat occurred, unbolt and remove the rimmed flat and replace it with another set. Three Grand Prix teams used the idea; one was Renault which won the first French GP by posting rather incredible speeds of 92.4 mph for the flying kilometer and nearly 63 mph average for the race. The Renaults required fewer tire changes than other teams, as many as 11 in one case.

In the years to come, the battle of big-engined, heavy cars versus small-engined, lighter ones raged on. Proponents on both sides championed their ideas and both camps have had successes to draw upon as proof that they were correct. Racing regulations governed engine size, in most cases, yet there have always been clever ways around the rules, mostly by advances in technology that derived increasingly better all-around cars.

The search for the winning edge, not just in bigger, more-powerful engines, has always challenged racing-car builders to improve every aspect of their cars to achieve the maximum efficiency from the least weight.

True, an engine is the heart of a car and has received by far the majority of attention, yet engines have also benefited from the concept of the most horsepower from the least weight. Just as car-body design has steadily improved with decreased aerodynamic drag, engine design has benefited from reduced internal friction and improved airflow in and out of combustion chambers.

The continual development of better brakes, cooling systems, tires, transmissions, carburetion, ignitions, materials and all other aspects of automotive engineering and technology have made auto racing the testbed for the ideas that have continually improved motoring in general.

REFINING GRAND PRIX CARS

In a few years, large and heavy cars like this Grand Prix Benz became a thing of the past. But for 1908, they were among the fiercest of competitors. Road & Track photo.

During the early days of motorcars, there were very few prior designs to draw upon. Thus, a transition of supporting technology from other applications to automobiles was required. This lack of background technology gave creative designers a "clean slate" to begin with, and many advances were made mainly through trial and error. Early-day designs progressively separated automobiles from their beginnings as motored carriages to road-going machines in their own right.

Leading the way through this remarkably innovative era was the development of ever more sophisticated engines. How to get increasingly more power from progressively smaller and more reliable engines was surely the prime mover in the technical development of the automobile. All other aspects of motored travel, however clever, original and noteworthy, were in support of the quest for *more speed*.

Racing improved the breed, and throughout the early history of automobiles, a continuous lineage of improvements built upon prior improvements to achieve what racing-car designers and builders hoped would be their winning edge. The winners became history and losers mostly forgotten, although successful ideas and innovations were developed by both winners and losers.

Winners have always captured the imagination of the public, and the ire of losers, and if a designer was astute, he would try to learn as much as possible from winning cars to make his own designs better. Consequently, the evolution of cars, and more specifically the development of racing cars, has been the product of a vast interchange of ideas combined with moments of inspiration on the part of many automotive pioneers.

When reading the history of automobiles, it soon becomes apparent that as time goes on, fewer and fewer really new ideas have been made. The reason is that most of that ground was covered in the first 30 years of automotive development; a time when designers could be individually creative.

GRAND PRIX BENZ
1908

12.5-liter/762.5-CID in-line 4-cylinder
120 HP @ 1500 rpm
Over 2725 lb, open body, leaf-spring suspension

Two illustrative examples of automotive technology early on will show the diversity of ideas and the rapidity of change. They are the Grand Prix Benz of 1908 and the Grand Prix FIAT of 1921.

First the Benz. From the age of iron, the big, heavy Benz emerged to be a feared competitor on many tracks in both Europe and America. But by 1904, a young and innovative technical team was in place at the old and staid Benz company in Mannheim, and they produced a light and fast racing car. From that the Benz technical team worked vigorously on a number of high-quality production cars and beyond them into racing cars that were campaigned by the Benz racing department.

Karl Benz, the 1880s pioneer, was opposed to innovation and regarded competition as unnecessary and abusive. He disapproved of the company's turn in direction and left the concern in 1906 to start his own works to produce cars he preferred.

With the old man gone, the Mannheimers set to serious race-car designing. Victor Hemery, a fearsome fellow noted for his temper and strength, joined the established Benz design team in 1907. His 11 years of experience with noted French auto builders, Bollec and Darracq, won him a ranking position and later the job of manhandling the cars in competition as noted earlier.

Even with the youthful design team in control, the resulting Benz Grand Prix car used a massive four-cylinder engine displacing 15 liters. A four-speed gearbox delivered power to a hefty sprocket and chain drive. Seating was high with the overall shape of the car being boxy and massive in character.

Contrasting that heaviness were the FIAT GP cars of 1921—23. They came, proved their supremacy, then left the tracks and returned to Grand Prix racing again only briefly. The FIATs became the most consistently successful cars for a generation of motor racing and left a rich legacy of ideas that inspired racing-car design for generations to come. When FIAT management chose to withdraw from racing, the brilliant racing-car design team broke up to find positions with other concerns which were doing exciting work.

By the early 1920s, Grand Prix racing rules began to limit engine

Christian Lautenschlager won the Grand Prix of Dieppe of 1908 in a 12.8-liter, chain-driven Mercedes by averaging 69 mph for 477 miles. In 1914, he drove this 4.5-liter car to win the Grand Prix at Lyons with an average of 65.83 mph for 466 miles. One of these cars also won the 1915 Indianapolis 500. Author photo courtesy of the Briggs Cunningham Automotive Museum.

displacement, thereby encouraging smaller, ligher cars. For example, in 1921, the limit for GP cars was 3 liters. FIAT's response to this was to develop a trend-setting in-line eight-cylinder engine. The FIAT Type 801 was an entirely original concept using two valves per cylinder, a crankshaft with 10-roller main bearings and roller rod bearings. Attention to balancing allowed reliable revs to a previously unheard of 4400 rpm. It was to dominate Grand Prix engine design for years to come.

The following year, displacement was further limited to 2 liters. FIAT used six of the eight cylinders of the 801, then reduced the stroke. This engine produced 92 HP at 4500 rpm and was so mechanically efficient it easily exceeded the potential of its rivals. Demonstrating this fact was Felice Nazzaro in the French GP that year where he finished nearly an hour ahead of the next contender, one of a trio of Bugattis that were the only other finishers.

The FIAT engine was upgraded for the next race, on the new Monza circuit, which promised very high speeds. The engine produced 112 HP at a reliable 5500 rpm and drivers were cleared to use 5000 rpm.

Paul Daimler designed this 1914 GP engine, an overhead-cam 4-cylinder that produced 115 HP at 2900 rpm from 4.5 liters. Specific output had risen to 25.56 HP/liter and shows the rapid advances made in racing-engine design. Author photo courtesy of the Briggs Cunningham Automotive Museum.

Cockpit treatment changed little over the early years of racing. Just the basics then and now. However, handling became easier with lighter cars. This 1914 model weighed 2,400 pounds unladen. Author photo courtesy of the Briggs Cunningham Automotive Museum.

The FIATs were so superior that most other teams forfeited their entry fees to jeers of cowardice rather than prove their ineptitude. Maserati and Bugatti, however, did run but FIAT performed as expected and won by cruising to a record victory.

FIAT engineers were thoroughly efficient in producing a complete car. Extensive aerodynamic detailing throughout the car presented the minimum frontal area and least drag showing that, at least at FIAT, attention was being paid to improvements in all areas.

The 1922 six-cylinder engine was just an interim step to the FIAT engine that set the principles for GP racing for the next 30 years. It was a straight-8, the first *supercharged* GP car. At the French GP of '23, the 130-HP FIAT ran a lap record of 87.75 mph, but dust picked up in the induction of the car's unscreened supercharger sidelined the car, letting the FIAT-inspired Sunbeam of Henry O. D. Segrave win with an average speed of 75.3 mph.

Tempers flared over this oversight and resulted in FIAT design-team member Luigi Bazzi's departure. He was a good friend of Alfa Romeo driver, Enzo Ferrari, who introduced him to the Alfa racing department. Once with Alfa, Bazzi suggested that Vittorio Jano be lured away from FIAT. Ferrari was sent to do this, and he was successful. With such talent reinforcing Alfa's racing-car design group, carbon-copies of both the six- and eight-cylinder FIAT engines were produced. The straight-8 eventually emerged in the all-conquering P2 Alfa Romeo of later years.

Meanwhile, FIAT replaced the vane-type supercharger on their first supercharged cars with a Roots-type, added intercoolers and fitted stone guards among other lesser improvements. The FIAT team continued to dominate GP racing with eight-cylinder cars producing 146 HP and weighing about 1450 pounds—for a while.

GRAND PRIX MERCEDES
1914

4.5-liter/274.5-CID SOHC in-line 4-cylinder
115 HP @ 2900 rpm
2400 lb, open body, leaf-spring suspension

But in the mid- to late '20s, FIAT began to back away from racing. Ideas so soundly displayed in the FIAT found their way into all sorts of other cars, and with the breakup of the FIAT team, other manufacturers picked up some of the best proven talent available. However, that was not all to be heard from FIAT.

The last racing FIAT was the Type 806 of 1927. This was a twelve-cylinder, 1.5-liter car that gave 187 HP at 8500 rpm. It was entered in one race, the Milan GP of 1927, and easily won. Again proving FIAT's ability to design, race and win against the most sophisticated racing cars in the world, the 806 left the Grand Prix scene and was never heard from again, and neither was FIAT on GP circuits.

MERCER RACEABOUT

This 1912 Mercer Raceabout shows an unusual color—light blue. At the time, such a color was considered devilish, an unpopular association. Author photo courtesy of the Briggs Cunningham Automotive Museum.

In the early days of public motoring, cars were expensive and owned mainly by the sporting wealthy. The upper crust still clung to the stately tradition of horse and carriage as the only proper way to travel. A lack of regulations governing the driving of cars created animosity from non-drivers. It was the age of dust and glory; true to advertisements showing cars at what appeared to be supersonic speeds, motorists amused themselves with the glory of driving as fast as they could and gave the dust to everything they passed.

Were it not for the advent of asphalt highways, the growth of the automobile industry would likely have suffered due to widespread adverse opinion.

In racing, it took sheer courage to overtake another car. Vast dust clouds billowed behind a speeding car and engulfed everything to the rear. Racing required drivers to face the dust and strong-arm their

ill-handling, ungainly cars, and court disaster at every turn. Mechanics were of iron constitution, too, for they had little to hold on to. It is no wonder that the first decade of motoring has come to be known as the "Heroic Age."

With such demands placed on racing, one would have done well to choose a Mercer Raceabout. Introduced in 1910 as the Speedster, the Mercer was an advanced design for its time; small, trim, reasonably light and powerful enough to stay ahead of other cars. Being quality built with a sporty low-slung appearance from mounting the engine and gearbox low for better handling, the Mercer Speedster looked every bit the meaning of its name.

Ferdinand and Charles Roebling—the Brooklyn Bridge Roeblings—and Anthony and John Kuser were among the cream of Trenton, New Jersey, society. They founded their company in May, 1909 and started building Mercers. One of their first products, the L-head "30," used a magneto/coil ignition system and Stromberg carburetor on an in-line four-cylinder engine capable of producing 34 HP and 60 mph.

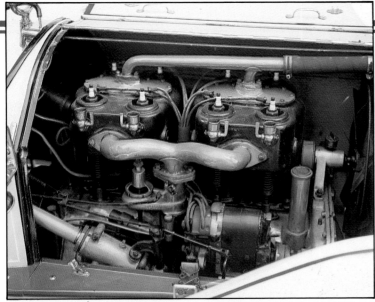

The 4.7-liter Mercer T-head engine was guaranteed to produce 58 HP and could rev to 1800 rpm. Powering an open car of around 2450 lb, speeds of over 75 mph were achieved in normal tune. Author photo courtesy of the Briggs Cunningham Automotive Museum.

Another feature of note was the use of drum brakes on the rear wheels that employed both internal and external brake shoes.

In its first racing appearance, a "30" took an improbable victory in a lengthy 16-hour bout that ended in the night after both leading cars, Mercer and Overland, had lost their lights.

Perhaps the masterpiece Mercer is the T-head Type 35 Raceabout of 1911. The "T" designation originated from the shape of the combustion chamber, a "T" shape with chambers on either side at the top of the bore for dual sparkplugs. Designer Finley Robertson Porter gave his Mercers graceful good looks combined with substantial performance and stamina. Many drivers achieved fame with them and imparted legendary status to the line.

Porter's "T" engine was an internal two-cam (in the block) design; one cam operated intake valves on the right while the other worked exhaust valves on the left. High contour cams for quick opening valves gave the engine high volumetric efficiency. Pistons were of gray iron with fully balanced high-strength steel connecting rods. The hefty crankshaft with 2-in. diameter main bearings was also balanced, to 1800 rpm, and rode in three bronze-layered, white-brass bearings. An oil pump force-fed oil galleries which drained to the main bearings, while rod-bearing lubrication was by the more conventional splash technique.

The requirement that each engine produce 58 HP on Mercer's dynamometer ensured that the cars delivered good performance. Porter's design and dynamic balancing helped provide vibration-free long life. Mercers also received three- or four-speed gearboxes made of high-quality material with gears machined for quiet operation. In both units,

third was direct while fourth was overdrive in the four-speed. In normal tune, a T-head Raceabout would do about 75 mph, an incredible speed for its day. With only 286 cubic inches (4.7 liters), Mercer T-head engines were decidedly small by comparison to other cars.

Overall weight of a Raceabout topped out at around 2450 pounds, also decidedly below competitors, and the superb combination of engine and gearbox in the Raceabout's well-balanced chassis produced a natural racing car. Porter believed that racing improved the breed. He stated that weaknesses in a design of a car might not show up at all in normal use but would surface in a single day at top speed.

MERCER RACEABOUT
1912

4.7-liter/286-CID twin internal-cam in-line 4-cylinder
58 HP @ 1800 rpm
2450 lb, open body, leaf-spring suspension

The T-head Mercer took its first win in February, 1911, and soon afterward the decision was made to enter the Indy 500. Plans were laid to take the T-head up to 300 cubic inches, just over half the displacement of the favored 597-CID (9.8-liter) Simplex of Ralph DePalma or the 583-CID (9.6-liter) Mercedes of Spencer Wishart. Two Raceabouts fresh off the street were entered among 44 other entrants. Works drivers Charles Bigelow and Britisher Hughie Hughes drove their cars flat-out and averaged 63 mph to take 12th and 15th finishes. And they did so without raising their cars' hoods a single time!

In becoming the most talked about cars in America, Hughes took race after race with Mercers. One was Savannah's Challenge Trophy, a 223-mile race where Hughes averaged 68.25 mph to win by over six minutes against his nearest challenger.

DePalma, who became Mercer's most celebrated driver, came over to Mercer and opened the 1912 season with a blitz. DePalma, Hughes, Eddie Pullen and other Mercer drivers scored many wins with DePalma setting several Class-C speed records that gave Mercer international acclaim. Back to Indy in 1912, a Mercer racer scored a spectacular third with an average of 76.3 mph among 24 starters, most with double the displacement such as the winning National.

Through 1914, Mercer scored resounding successes until two Mercers locked wheels in a passing maneuver that sent Spencer Wishart to his death. The factory announced shortly afterward that their racing was ended. Although Pullen went on to win what became known as the greatest race ever held on the west coast, at Corona, California, November of 1914, in a thrilling photo finish against Barney Oldfield in a Maxwell, the golden days of Mercer racing were over. Porter left the company in 1915, which saw some redirection under his replacement. Although later Mercers were raced and attained speeds of 95.2 mph, the glory days were finished.

THE RISE OF SPORTS CARS

The 1912 Hispano-Suiza 15T roadster is considered by many to be the first true sports car, although that term had not been invented at the time. The car so impressed King Alphonso XIII of Spain, that he personally endorsed the car. At 2250 lb with almost 50/50 weight distribution, the 15T was nimble and fun to drive. Author photo courtesy of the Briggs Cunningham Automotive Museum.

In 1899, the Fabbrica Italiana Automobili Torino (F.I.A.T.) was formed. Shortly thereafter, a small but successful firm was acquired that employed both Vincenzo Lancia and Felice Nazzaro, two names that were to figure prominently in auto history. Lancia and Nazzaro formed FIAT's first racing team with Lancia driving for 10 years through 1910. FIAT's racing fortunes grew as Lancia's technical brilliance shown, but in 1906 Lancia left to form his own company, Fabbrica Automobili Lancia e Cia.

Lancia was obsessed with road-holding, braking and reliability, three aspects known of a number of the cars that carried his name. He continually filed for patents on his innovative chassis ideas while always looking for improvements.

Lancia models became designated by the letters of the Greek alphabet with the Tipo 51 becoming known as the "Alfa," a phonetic

Mark Birkigt designed the 15T and produced this T-head 3.6-liter four-cylinder (80 X 180mm bore and stroke). Intake valves on the right are operated by a camshaft located on the right of the cast-aluminum crankcase. Exhaust valves on the left are operated by another cam located on the left side of the block. Power is 64 HP at 2300 rpm. Author photo courtesy of the Briggs Cunningham Automotive Museum.

Functional cockpit of the Hispano-Suiza 15T provided refined motoring in a responsive package. Author photo courtesy of the Briggs Cunningham Automotive Museum.

Millions of Model T Fords were built. With such availability, they became the basis of a variety of racing machines such as this Ascot dirt racer. Drivers sat high in their *bobtail* racers.

spelling of the Greek Alpha. In an interesting quirk of racing-car development, the "Alfa" was criticized for being too fast and too light with a too-high-revving engine, a 2543cc four-cylinder developing 28 HP at 1800 rpm. It could reach 58 mph in fourth gear.

Following World War I and rapid growth at Lancia, a 22° V8 and 22° V12 were developed, although the public was not ready for them. Overhead valves with a single overhead cam on each bank appeared on the V12. That engine displaced 6 liters (366 CID) and developed 90 HP at 2200 rpm, a remarkable achievement for 1919.

A sporting-version Lancia, the Dikappa, with overhead valves, appeared in 1921. Its wooden "torpedo" body clothed in aluminum sheet produced a light car that could whisk along at 87 mph from 87 HP.

Lancia built a wide variety of vehicles, some with big engines like those found in a variety of cars in both Europe and America. Examples are the 16-liter (976-CID) Locomobile that won the Vanderbilt Cup in 1906, all the cars filling the first ten places of the 1911 Indianapolis 500 led by a 7.3-liter Marmon Wasp or the "small-engine" Stutz Bearcat at 6.4 liters (390 cubic inches) in 11th place. Another is Italy's elegant Isotta-Fraschini 12-liter Racing Runabout of 1910.

However, amid all the monster-size engines of the time, a tradition was building among small-engine cars. The Duesenberg brothers had noticed the third-place finish of a 300-CID Mercer at Indy in 1912 and were encouraged that a light car could run with the giants. That began their tradition with the famed *walking beam* engine of about 230 cubic inches that scored many wins.

Just as Lancia and other European car builders were finding the light car exciting and competitive, so were their American counterparts. In the days to come, teams from both continents would meet on tracks around the world to prove their cars against each other in competition.

HISPANO-SUIZA ALPHONSO XIII
1912

3.6-liter/220-CID twin internal-cam in-line 4-cylinder
64 HP @ 2300 rpm
2215 lb, open body, leaf-spring suspension

On local levels in America, Henry Ford's Model T built an enormous following as all sorts of aftermarket items became available. The stripped down dirt trackers and their Model T racers are one type, while the Speedster conversion was popular among those who retained the full-bodied look. These aftermarket bodies replaced the Ford-built body with a lowered, two-place speedster. The glamour and publicity produced by the sporting image of these cars, and their speeds of over 45 mph, no doubt influenced T sales to the tune of 1,788,477 cars in 1922.

Lightweight, nimble, responsive, small engine, two-place, spirited and visibly well balanced: These were among the features in the development of a particular sort of car in the 'teens and early '20s. They were the cars with appeal, a certain attractive charisma. They were the works of art that created love affairs with automobiles and "spoke" with a beckoning to be driven. Those were the cars that were so satisfying to drive that once behind the wheel, one wanted to drive for the sheer pleasure of it.

The term *sports car* had not been invented at the time, but it was clear that cars of the sporting kind had a universal, timeless appeal. Perhaps the first sports car was the Hispano-Suiza 15T designed by Marc Birkigt. This car was also known as the Alphonso XIII, so named for the

14

All sorts of racing equipment was offered to Model T racers including double overhead cam conversions. This particular engine has been set up similarly with an aluminum (Post WWII) cylinder head to what the average dirt racer could have built in the early 1920s, a basically stock block with a special head, twin carbs and stub exhaust pipes.

Removal of all unnecessary hardware resulted in a light but sturdy racing car. Note the stock Model T frame, front suspension and hand fuel pump.

young king of Spain who officially endorsed the car when it first appeared in 1912. It had all the features of a sports car and was designed for the sheer pleasure of driving.

FORD MODEL-T ASCOT RACER
1924

in-line 4-cylinder, power dependent on modification
Frontenac 16-valve, chain-driven DOHC conversion available
stripped Model T, less than 900 lb

On the other end of the scale, there were cars that can be called tiny, the Austin 7 for instance. Herbert Austin, later to become knighted as Sir Herbert Austin, was the force behind the 7. He called it his "baby car" and its size shows it is indeed described correctly.

Austin was an automotive pioneer and designed his first car in 1896. Born in Britain, Austin spent the decade between his 17th and 27th years in Australia with the Wolesley Sheep Shearing Company. His obvious technical expertise won him the position of engineer, but it was those long, arduous treks through the outback that firmed up his conviction that there had to be a more civilized way of traveling.

First a proponent of engines of the horizontal design while with the automotive branch of Vickers Sons and Maxim, British ship builders, Austin left the firm over arguments with other directors when cars with

Cord-wrapped stock Model T steering wheel provided good grip.

vertical engines were introduced. In 1905, Austin formed his own company, the Austin Motor Company. When his first cars appeared in 1906, all 147 of them built had vertical engines! Apparently his disagreements at Vickers was an excuse to leave.

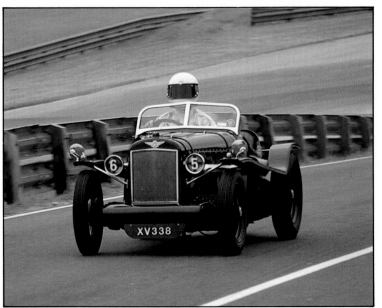

Small almost to the extreme, Brooklands Sports Racers weighed just 875 lb and were built on a wheelbase of only 6 feet.

Sir Herbert Austin saved his failing automobile manufacturing firm with the diminutive Austin 7. It was a hugh sales success and became the Model T of Britain. Brooklands factory racing cars like this one were highly competitive in small-engine classes.

AUSTIN 7 BROOKLANDS SPORTS RACER
1928

0.75-liter/45.6-CID in-line 4-cylinder
20 HP @ 2600 rpm
875 lb, aluminum body, leaf-spring suspension

Austin's works grew tremendously through World War I, from 2000 to 22,000 employees. But afterward, the general economic climate in Great Britain was depressed. Austin car production had reached 2246 units in 1921, but it was in that year that his company nearly failed and was placed in receivership. Times were tough and to survive intact required bold moves.

Austin was just the man. His outback tenacity training as a young man prevailed at the time he needed it most. His Austin 20 was criticized as too American, too big, and as sales declined in 1921, prices climbed 40 percent. A scaled-down version of the 20, known as the 12, was not able to provide the necessary recovery. It was under these sorts of pressures that Austin conceived the diminutive 7.

His proposal was not well received by other company directors, but Sir Herbert never looked back. From his car drawing office, he selected 17-year-old Stanley Edge to work with him at home to complete the design of the 7 in the shortest time possible. It was done in eight months. The result was a tiny four-place car continuing the quality Austins were noted for but in a car so small it had to be inexpensive.

The Austin 7 was indeed a bold move, but it proved to be exactly on the mark as the line became Britain's most famous and sold some

300,000 units before the model was dropped in 1939. What Henry Ford's Model T did for Americans, the Austin 7 did for middle-class Britons. It put them on affordable wheels.

Because they were popular and easy to own, an entire aftermarket industry grew up in support of the sporting-minded who wanted to race. The 7 platform provided many backyard tinkerers the opportunity to experiment with their own ideas for cars. Both Colin Chapman's first Lotus and John Cooper's first special were built upon modifications of the 7.

Sir Herbert himself sent his cars into the fray because he was convinced that competition disclosed problems early on and was productive testing. The first 7, as a prototype, went hillclimbing and secured a third in class the first time out. Once in production, high sales of 7s brought continuing good fortunes for Austin and led to the advent of factory racing cars, for instance the Brooklands Sports Racers of 1928.

Lines of these two-place roadsters were basically scaled down from larger Austin cars with conventional styling of the early 1920s.

Austin 7 four-cylinder engine was air-cooled and displaced only 748cc (45.6 cubic inches). Car would do 60 mph.

Austin commissioned six of these cars from E. C. Gordon England, who had his shop near the famed Brooklands track. The cars looked the same with their trim roadster bodies, but were fitted with engines in various states of tune and development. One was supercharged, another had twin carburetors, a third had higher compression and no fan or water pump while the remaining three ran other combinations.

Just 8-feet, 8-inches long and on a wheelbase of 6 feet, these tiny cars weighed only 875 pounds. That was due largely to aluminum bodies and the use of Austin 7 engines and transmissions also made of aluminum. They were built on Austin 7 frames and running gear for the purpose of showing the reliability and performance potential of Austin's products.

The Austin 7 Brooklands Sports Racers took the idea of sporting cars almost to the smallest possible extreme, yet they were highly competitive and very popular. While among the tiniest of four-cylinder production engines ever built, the little cars' 748cc (45.6-CID) power-plants were able to propel them along at a spritely 60 miles per hour. Supercharged models and those with dual carbs, high-lift cams and other racing preparation were able to compete reliably to around 90 mph.

Although not terribly exciting by the standards of the big-engine set, these cars gained a huge following because people could afford them and many Austin 7s competed in speed events.

Most events stressed reliability rather than high speeds, and hill-climbs, rallys and other such club-sponsored outings were the source of competition for most people. With the number of Austin 7s built, one can conclude that many people got their first racing experiences behind the wheels of these tiny cars.

The Brooklands Sports Racer models proved themselves in all sorts of races as Austin factory racers. One of the 1929 models, also built by Gordon England, won Britain's equivalent of the Indy 500 at Brooklands and clearly proved the potential of small cars powered by small engines, an idea that was here to stay.

BUGATTI

Legendary Bugatti straight-8 Type 35 appeared first in 1924. At first a 2-liter car (66 X 88mm bore and stroke), the Type 35 went through several variations and accounted for more than 1500 claimed victories during its production lifetime through 1931.

could simplify a complex of mutually interfering components into obvious beauty.

Many of the parts he designed were drawn free-hand, and they rarely failed. That was because he understood the action of mechanical

The true sports car has, on occasion, been described as a lightly detuned and only slightly more streetable version of a Grand Prix racing car. Fitting this description were the sensational French cars of Ettore Bugatti. Based on a remarkable philosophy and his extraordinary talent, Bugatti built cars that made indelible marks in the history of racing.

To single-handedly design a successful car, one should be a master of all necessary phases of science, engineering and manufacturing. Ettore Bugatti was none of these. An artist who was a master of proportion, he had the wisdom to surround himself with talented engineers whom he paid well but demanded total anonymity. The fact that many of his designs have become overwhelmingly celebrated as among the greatest ever achieved provides credit to his creative genius, a genius that

GRAND PRIX BUGATTI TYPE 35
1924

2-liter/122-CID supercharged in-line SOHC 8-cylinder
135 HP @ 5000 rpm
under 1652 lb, aluminum body, leaf-spring suspension

forces and the characteristics of metal, not because he calculated from theory or expressed his understanding in mathematics.

His first masterpiece, the 2-liter Type 35, appeared at the French Grand Prix of 1924. It was limited by failing tires to a best placing of

The classic Grand Prix Bugatti, the Type 51: This was the ultimate 2.3-liter supercharged Bugatti and came in response to increased pressure from Alfa Romeo. Forty were built between 1931 and 1935.

Type 51 Bugatti featured a DOHC head, rather than SOHC, with improved valve placement inspired by the Miller design. Power increased to a maximum 180 HP. Specific output became 78.26 hp/liter.

seventh overall. Bugatti, however, emerged as a serious Grand Prix challenger that year when his T-35 shown in the Spanish GP by finishing second just 90 seconds behind a Sunbeam. (This was the last British GP win on the continent until Tony Brooks won at Syracuse in a Connaught in 1955.)

A Type 35 set a lap record of 69.7 mph at San Sebastian, and for the following seven years less one, Type 35s dominated Grand Prix racing. Unfortunately, spreading economic depression and rapid rule changes without consistent enforcement produced a period of steady decline of interest in GP racing.

The Type 35 was conceived in the midst of all of this as a production racing car. Its intention was to sell in large enough numbers to earn a profit but at a price to attract amateur racers. To do so required the cars to be models of efficient design. That is, simple in every detail, and both rugged and reliable in addition to being powerful enough to win, or at least durable enough to survive to the end. What the T-35 did was to become one of the winningest racing cars ever built and claimed more than 1500 victories during its production lifetime of 1924 to 1931.

Their creator, Bugatti the man, was a keen observer who was able to adapt ideas to his own cause. For instance, the springs-through-the-front-axle idea came from the 1922 Grand Prix FIAT. Another idea came from America's famed engine and race-car builder, Harry Miller.

Bugatti first built engines with a rather unconventional three-valve-per-cylinder OHC valve-train layout with an odd cylinder-wall location for sparkplugs. Miller's design inspired him to produce a far-better two-valve, twin-cam head for the Type 50 and later cars. Bugatti wins continued with engines of this type, including LeMans 1937 and '39 with a streamlined Type 57SC. (The latter was a 3.25-liter car that Wimille and Veyron drove to the highest average speed and greatest distance

covered in pre-World War II LeMans 24-Hours events: 86.86 mph for 2084.54 miles.)

The last of the boat-tail Grand Prix Bugattis was the Type 59 of 1933. It began as a 2.8-liter straight-8 of 230 HP then went to 3.3 liters and 240 HP in 1934. The reason for the T-59 was to counter the Alfa Romeo P3 Monoposto cars that eclipsed the Type 51 Bugatti in 1932. The Type 59 was an improvement on the Type 35, but down on power compared to adversaries.

Following illustrious careers of the Type 35 and 51 GP cars, Type 59 Bugattis took only two Grand Prix victories and three lesser wins and have been variously acclaimed or criticized since then depending on one's perspective. What it did not do was restore Bugatti's lost fame. The dreaded Alfas of the brilliant Italian Vittorio Jano were overpowering.

GRAND PRIX BUGATTI TYPE 51
1932

2.3-liter/140-CID supercharged in-line DOHC 8-cylinder
130 HP @ 5500 rpm
under 1652 lb, aluminum body, leaf-spring suspension

Along the way to the Type 59 came a huge variety of Bugatti cars from small to very large. The theme of a sports car being a slightly detuned version of a Grand Prix car was expressed well in Grand Sport Bugattis. Two of note were the Type 43 and Type 55.

The immortal Type 35B Grand Prix Bugatti became the basis of the Type 43 Grand Sport in 1927. Intended for road use, the Type 43 was the

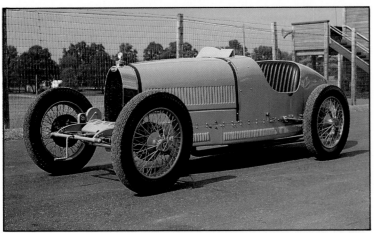

A 1.5-liter voiturette Bugatti Type 37 was introduced in 1927 for the amateur racer and became highly popular. Classic lines of the Grand Prix Bugatti were evident in all racing cars derived from the Type 35.

In four-cylinder form, the Type 37 engine compartment looks a bit bare. A single Solex carburetor feeds through two intake valves and one sparkplug per cylinder fires the mixture. A single exhaust valve clears the combustion chamber with peak power about 60 HP. About 95 mph was on tap.

For Ettore Bugatti, weight was the enemy. Full-bore supercharged Type 35 Grand Prix cars weighed just 1650 lb, while the Type 37 Sports models with cycle fenders and headlamps weighed somewhat less. Production records show 290 Type 37s were built.

BUGATTI TYPE 37 SPORTS
1927

1.5-liter/92-CID in-line 4-cylinder
60 HP @ 4500 rpm
1600 lb, aluminum body, leaf-spring suspension

first Bugatti adapted from a successful racing chassis and carried over many virtues of the GP car's performance and handling.

The highly acclaimed boat-tail Type 35 ran the Bugatti-patented eight-spoke alloy wheels with integral steel-lined brake hubs on all four wheels. The car's cable-operated brakes were very effective, and all cars were built on a wheelbase of 7 feet, 10.5 inches. The Type 43, a two-place

rumble-seat roadster, received a 9-foot, 1/2-inch wheelbase and similar equipment.

As mentioned earlier, the unusual eight-cylinder Type 35 engine was a three-valve design, with two inlets and one exhaust, using a single overhead camshaft and a five-main roller-bearing crankshaft lubricated by a gear-driven pump. Later supercharged models, such as the 35B, ran a Roots blower driven at engine speed and mounted low to the right alongside the engine. These cars used a single Zenith carburetor, while unblown cars were fitted with two Solex carbs. Output of unblown engines topped at about 110 HP while supercharged models delivered

The first time this technique had been used was by Emile Petit of the Societe des Moteurs Salmson who had produced a somewhat similar design in 1928, the 1085cc Salmson eight-cylinder that produced 140 HP at 8000 rpm. However, history does not record whether or not Jano was influenced by the French design. In any case, the Salmson was not seriously developed, and Jano's engine was. Thus, it was Jano who proved the principles of the design in world-class competition, and history duly records his great accomplishments.

ALFA ROMEO 6C 1750 GRAN SPORT
1931

1.75-liter/107-CID twin-overhead cam 6-cylinder
85 HP @ 4500 rpm
2025 lb, roadster by Zagato, leaf-spring suspension

A total of 257 6C 1750 Alfas were built through 1933 when they were replaced by the even more dominant 8C 2300.

During the rise of the immortal P2, Alfa Romeo had determined that a potentially lucrative market existed for high-performance sports cars. Jano responded with his 6C 1500 that appeared in prototype form in 1925. This car, with its single-overhead-cam six, was the beginning of an equally brilliant line of sports cars to accompany Alfa's Grand Prix cars. In 1928, the production 1500 Sport appeared with twin overhead cams and hemispherical combustion chambers, producing 54 HP and achieving top speeds over 75 mph. Next came the more exciting 6C 1500 Super

By far the most successful of Vittorio Jano's six-cylinder designs, the 6C 1750 displaced 1752cc from a bore and stroke of 65 X 88mm. Supercharged with a compression ratio of 5:1, output of the twin cam was 85 HP at 4500 rpm.

Sport on a shorter wheelbase and lighter weight with its high-compression engine producing 76 HP at 4800 rpm.

In 1928, Campari and Giulio Ramponi won the famed Mille Miglia in a 6C 1500, the only such car entered, and showed the capability of Alfa Romeo sports cars. Soon, the 1500 gave way to the legendary 6C 1750. The 1750 Sport was succeeded by the Super Sport and the top of the range became the Gran Sport. The open cars in supercharged form produced 85 HP and could reach 90 mph. When produced in closed form, a new name was needed, thus the 1750 Gran Turismo. The factory team car produced 102 HP and could top 105 mph, with excellent handling and acceleration to match.

These 1750 Alfas were the best sports cars of their time. Campari and Ramponi won the 1929 Mille Miglia, and Tazio Nuvolari repeated the win the next year while beating his arch-rival, Achille Varzi.

Although unable to beat Bugatti in the Targa Florio for a number of years, that Sicilian mountain challenge soon became another Alfa Romeo circuit with the advent of the 8C 2300 sports car.

These cars were designed from the beginning to be sports cars and thus received all of the attention necessary to produce a well-rounded car. Its engine, a new eight-cylinder, soon began another illustrious racing career.

A variety of cars was produced on different wheelbases. The "Two-Three" was a 122-inch version with a long hood and swooping fenders leading from the front wheels. Everything about this big car was strong and built for the purpose of endurance racing. Competition 2300s were built on a 108.3-inch wheelbase.

Between the Grand Prix P2 Alfa and the overwhelming P3 came the 8C 2600 Monza. These were versatile cars that could be raced as sports cars with cycle fenders and lighting or as Grand Prix cars without such equipment.

Six Monzas were built using equipment from eight-cylinder sports cars. The name is in honor of their first victory, the 1932 Grand Prix of Europe at Monza, where two cars led across the finish line.

The "Two-Three" engine had finned intake manifolds for an intercooler effect between the supercharger and hemispherical combustion chambers. Both four-cylinder blocks were of light alloy and were mounted on an aluminum crankcase. Light-alloy pistons rode on machined steel connecting rods. Both steel crankshafts were fully counterweighted and were held by a combined total of ten main bearings. Interchangeable cylinder heads, also of light alloy, were of cross-flow design with 90° inclined valves. Camshafts were drilled for lightness and ran in six plain bearings.

A racing version, the Spider Corsa 8C 2300 of 1931, produced 155 HP at 5200 rpm. In later developments, power went to 165, then to 180 HP at 5400 rpm in 1934. When displacement was bumped to 2900cc, the 8C 2900 delivered 220 HP in racing form and 180 as a tourer. Depending on which final-drive ratio was selected, the "Two-Three" was capable of between 115 and 129 mph in 1932. Its massive brakes could haul down the car with ease.

Jano's sports Alfas came on the LeMans scene to end the Bentley wins of the late 1920s. Two 8C 2300s were entered in 1931, one driven by Sir Henry Birkin who co-drove the winning Bentley in 1929. Bentley had won in 1924 and again in 1927, '28, '29 and 1930, showing that W. O. Bentley's cars were durability masters.

Birkin switched to Alfa Romeo in 1931 and with Lord Howe, their final hours of the race was a face-off against a big 7.1-liter, 225 HP Mercedes-Benz. Although the long Mulsanne Straight favored the brute speed of the Mercedes, the 2.3-liter Alfa Romeo relied on agility and stamina to post the first of four successive Alfa Romeo victories at

LeMans. The Birkin/Howe win in 1931 was the first time in LeMans history that 3000 kilometers (1864 miles) was surpassed in 24 hours. Their win set both speed and distance records, 78.13 mph for 1875.08 miles.

From the illustrious 8C 2300 sports car came Jano's second Grand Prix machine. The new short-wheelbase two-seater could be fitted with full fenders or cycle fenders and lights to run as a sports car. Two of these GP cars were run in the 1931 Grand Prix of Europe at Monza where they won with a 1-2 finish. After that, these Alfas became forever known as the "Monza."

ALFA ROMEO 8C 2300 MONZA
1933

2.3-liter/140-CID supercharged twin-overhead cam
in-line 8-cylinder
180 HP @ 5600 rpm
2020 lb dry, aluminum body, leaf-spring suspension

The Monza engine was developed from the "Two-Three" and proved to be another brilliant Jano design. His engine had gone full circle: The P2 Grand Prix eight-cylinder gave rise to the six-cylinder for sports cars that became the eight-cylinder "Two-Three" engine that was developed into another GP engine, the Monza.

Bore and stroke of the Monza, 65 X 88mm, produced 2336cc. Its crankcase was aluminum alloy fitted with steel cylinder liners and a detachable head with valves inclined at 90°. A large-capacity supercharger and single carburetor was located on the driver's right with exhaust to the left. Boost was about 8 pounds, and with a compression ratio of 6.5:1, output was 180 HP at 5600 rpm in 1933. Alcohol was the fuel of choice.

The Monza weighed just over 2000 pounds. On a wheelbase of 104 inches and a front/rear track of 55 inches, the car gave top speeds of 140 mph. With that sort of potential, Jano's Monza proved to be another

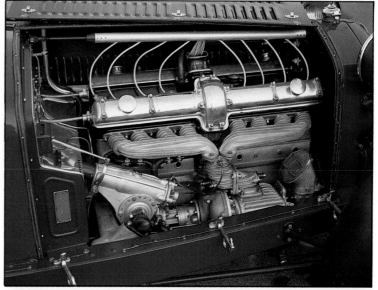

Another of Vittorio Jano's brilliant engine designs is this 8C 2300 Monza eight-cylinder. A single carburetor is mounted in front of a supercharger driven at 1.4 times engine speed. The compressed fuel/air mixture is intercooled while passing through the finned aluminum manifold. With a compression ratio of 6.5:1, power is 180 HP at 5600 rpm for a specific output of 78.26 HP/liter.

formidable Alfa Romeo.

In time, the P3, Jano's superb Grand Prix racer, proved dominant in the years between the Monza and the emergence of the all-conquering German GP cars.

GERMANY DOMINATES

Output of the Mercedes-Benz W154 increased to an unheard of 526 HP at 8000 rpm with the M163 engine for 1939. With that, W154 GP cars won the Grand Prix championship with Hermann Lang.

Auto Union, the union of four smaller German automobile manufacturers, produced rear-engine Grand Prix cars for Hitler's Nazi Germany. Designed by Dr. Ferdinand Porsche, and subsequently dubbed the P-Wagen in his honor, they were immensely innovative, most notably being rear-engine cars with independent suspension. Fred Puhn photo.

Grand Prix racing in the late '20s and early '30s experienced a severe loss of interest and was struggling to recapture its lost spirit from earlier years. The way that was achieved was politically motivated. Mussolini and Alfa Romeo is one example; another is Hitler's support of German racing cars.

The expense of Grand Prix racing had continually escalated beyond the scope of tinkerers with racing interests and was generally factory-supported efforts. Its prestige steadily rebuilt itself in the early 1930s as enthusiasts found ways, even if political in origin, to continue racing. Alfa wins had become worldwide conversation, and Ferdinand Porsche sought support for a car of his design to challenge the Italians

Awesome 6.1-liter supercharged V16 designed by Dr. Porsche turned out 520 HP at 5000 rpm in the Type C Auto Union of 1937. Block and heads are alloy with a single overhead camshaft between the cylinder heads. Transmission is a four-speed with a ZF limited-slip differential. Specific output is 85.25 HP per liter: power-to-weight ratio of 0.29 is comparable to Can-Am cars of the late '60s. Fred Puhn photo.

Grand Prix W154 Mercedes-Benz cars were built to the 1938—40 formula that specified 3-liter displacement for supercharged engines and 4.5 liters unsupercharged with a minimum weight of 850 kg (1874 lb). In 1939 form with the M163 engine, fuel consumption was around 2 miles per gallon. Therefore, to get increased range, they were fitted with tanks giving a fuel capacity of about 110 gallons. Fuel was mixture of methyl alcohol, nitrobenzene, acetone and sulphuric ether.

and gain international recognition.

He met with Hitler in 1933. Conversation centered on which German firm was to receive state funding for Grand Prix car development. Daimler-Benz seemed a sure bet, but Porsche argued for Auto Union and the importance of competing teams.

AUTO UNION TYPE C
1937

6.1-liter/372-CID supercharged overhead-cam V16
520 HP @ 5000 rpm
1814 lb dry, aluminum body on tubular frame,
independent suspension

Germany's new Chancellor wanted German GP wins, and Dr. Porsche grasped the occasion to champion the cause of carrying the new German ideology worldwide. In 1932, Dr. Porsche's private concern had completed his first designs of a revolutionary racing car, but funding was necessary to build it.

The Chancellor offered 600,000 Reichmarks to subsidize the cars, and although Hitler was leaning toward Daimler-Benz, Dr. Porsche convinced him that his design was ready to implement. With the pros-

pect of quick action, the decision was made to divide the funds equally between Auto Union and Daimler-Benz, much to the displeasure of D-B officials.

Out of the formula-libre rules, the 1930's equivalent of unlimited-displacement class racing, had come all sorts of cars that went faster and faster. To reduce speeds, new rules for the 1934 season placed a maximum weight of 750 kg (1652 lb) on cars, but placed no restriction on engines. The philosophy was that smaller cars would have smaller engines and consequently lower speeds. But the 750-kg formula proved just the opposite and provided the creative stimuli for unprecedented development of cars, particularly engines, that soon yielded the most-powerful cars ever seen.

It would be almost 35 years before their power per pound was surpassed. They were the German "blitzkrieg" cars mentioned earlier, the cars that overpowered all comers although Alfa Romeo managed to remain competitive in the hands of the incomparable Tazio Nuvolari while the German cars went through early development phases.

Both Auto Union and Daimler-Benz built cars to the 750-kg formula. The Daimler-Benz W25s were more conventional with a front-engine, eight-cylinder layout, while the Auto Union P-Wagen, named for Dr. Porsche, was a radical V16, rear-engine design that was immensely creative in every way. Some historians consider the Auto Union a mid-engine design because the engine was *ahead* of the rear axle.

The W25's supercharged 3.4-liters developed 314 HP. That in-

With 2654cc displacement (65 X 100mm bore and stroke), supercharged twin-cam Alfa Romeo P3 produced 215 HP at 5600 from twin carburetors and twin superchargers running at 1.448 times engine speed. Top speed was about 145 mph. Driver sat between twin prop shafts.

ALFA ROMEO P3
1932

2.65-liter/162-CID twin supercharged twin-overhead cam
in-line 8-cylinder
215 HP @ 5600 rpm
1540 lb unladen, single-seat aluminum body,
leaf-spring suspension, twin split prop shafts

creased to 462 HP at 5800 rpm in the 4.3-liter W25C as raced in 1935. The P-Wagen began with 4.5-liters and about 245 HP at 4500 rpm. That soon went to 350 HP, then 400. With later capacity increase to 6-liters, the P-Wagen jumped to 520 HP and the later W125 Grand Prix Mercedes-Benz of 1937 topped out at more than 600 HP, astounding power in a car of under 1600 pounds.

The German cars debuted in the 1934 season with indifferent results, although the famed Rudi Caracciola and Luigi Fagioli took the Italian GP in a W25. The '35 season saw the German tide reach its stride with the W-machines taking nine of Europe's major races. Caracciola, Mercedes' incomparable ace of aces, won five GPs, the Eifelrennen and became both the European and German champion, just two of his many championships in those years.

Alfa Romeo Monoposto Type B, or P3, was the ultimate in Vittorio Jano's Grand Prix designs. The P3 introduced as a 2.6-liter in 1932 went through three engine variations, eventually displacing 3.8 liters in the P3B of 1935.

Six P3 Alfas were built during 1932—33. Weighing just 1540 lb, their light-weight construction, excellent handling and braking enabled them to be competitive in the hands of top drivers like Tazio Nuvolari even though the Auto Unions and Mercedes-Benz GP cars were technically superior.

Because the W154 Mercedes-Benz carried so much fuel, over 700 pounds when topped off, the suspension was designed so that the driver could adjust shock valving to soften the ride during a race as fuel was used.

In Italy, Alfa Romeo had come under state control in 1933 and factory racing was ended as an unnecessary expense. Enzo Ferrari, director of Alfa's racing team, left to set up his own Scuderia to run the cars under the guise of "private" entries. Even though the silver German cars were increasingly more difficult to beat, a new version of the Alfa P3, the red P3B of Nuvolari out of Scuderia Ferrari, shown brilliantly in the 1935 German GP at Nurburgring and humbled the German pride on its home ground.

The lighter but underpowered P3B sporting an all-new 3.8-liter engine relied on nimble handling in the corners, and Nuvolari used that Alfa Romeo virtue to the fullest. Against the 462 HP, 4.3-liter W25Cs led by Caracciola and the 4.9-liter Type B Auto Unions led by Bernd Rosemeyer and Achille Varzi (who had recently joined Auto Union from Alfa), Nuvolari faced formidable odds but ran his greatest race.

The Nurburgring circuit was 14.2 miles of twisting Eifel mountain terrain, 22 laps and 312 miles in race length. On lap six, Nuvolari pressed past both a Mercedes-Benz and an Auto Union and pursued the flying Caracciola. By the 10th lap, his P3 led the next four leaders into the pits for fuel and tires. The efficient Germans got their cars out quickly, but after a disastrous 2-minute, 15-second pit stop, Nuvolari joined in sixth position.

MERCEDES-BENZ W154
1939

3-liter/183-CID overhead-cam in-line 8-cylinder
w/dual Roots blowers
526 HP @ 8000 rpm
1875 lb dry, aluminum body on tubular frame,
independent suspension

The leading Mercedes-Benz then set a new lap record trying to outstretch Nuvolari and fortune did indeed seem to favor its Prussian driver, Manfred von Brauchitsch, until the 20th lap when his right front tire wore through to the fiber. Nuvolari was after him like a man possessed. As the Mercedes slowed to protect its lead, a scant 32 seconds separated the two cars when, on the last lap and just 5 miles from the finish, the Mercedes' tire blew. Nuvolari shot by to win.

He had driven an incomparable race in the face of five Mercedes-Benz and four Auto Union cars, and even though the German spectators regretted the loss, they knew they had witnessed one of the all-time great drives in Grand Prix history.

The German GP that year was one among only a few losses the German Blitz gave up in the following years. It was clear to everyone that Reichmarks were overwhelming Grand Prix racing, and if other teams were to be competitive, another class was needed.

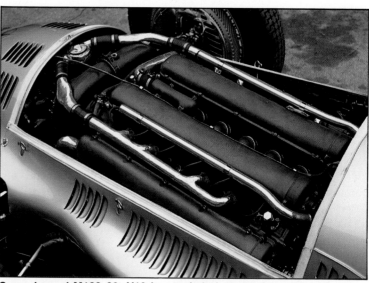

Supercharged M163 60° V12 is a technical masterpiece. Nine oil pumps ensure proper lubrication to the roller-bearing crankshaft at specific output of 175.3 HP per liter, among the highest of prewar cars.

VOITURETTES

Affectionately known as the *Alfetta*—little Alfa—the Tipo 158 did well in a variety of races although not in the Grande Epreuves (Grand Tests) of the Auto Union and Mercedes-Benz W154 league. The Tipo 158 provided the platform for World Championship Formula 1 racing after World War II.

In 1950, 350-HP Tipo 158s won 11 races in 11 starts with Giuseppe Farina taking the World Drivers Championship. Upgraded for 1951 as the Tipo 159, Alfa Romeo again won the World Championship while Juan Manuel Fangio, shown in his winning Alfetta, took the Drivers crown.

While GP racing became the battle ground of Auto Union versus Mercedes-Benz, other people who wanted to race in open-wheel formulas formed new classes or further developed those that already existed. Rather than weight limits, engine-capacity limits ensured competitiveness. One class limited engine size to 1.5 liters and with these smaller cars, many European builders saw some opportunity to race at speeds that promised considerable action. They were the prewar counterparts of later Formula-2 cars, and produced exciting racing in the form of small, single-seat roadsters.

Among many others, ERA (English Racing Automobile), Riley, AC and MG (Morris Garages) from England were joined by Maserati and Alfa Romeo while the French offered up their versions in a variety of specials with various engine sizes. Alfa introduced its Tipo 158. It was a line that became successful both before and after World War II.

After the war, Grand Prix racing adopted the 1.5-liter formula. Giuseppe Farina and Juan Manuel Fangio drove the 158s and their successors the Tipo 159, both supercharged cars, to back-to-back world driver championships in 1950 and '51 respectively. After 1951, Alfa Romeo dropped its Grand Prix racing efforts and stepped aside at a time when the fledgling Italian firm of Ferrari was just beginning to make its mark in motor racing.

The Tipo 159 Alfa Romeo supercharged in-line eight-cylinder (58 X 70mm bore and stroke) produced 420 HP at 9600 rpm. Double overhead cams were inclined at 100° with two valves and one sparkplug per cylinder. The two-stage Roots supercharger ran at 1.35 engine speed to develop 280 HP per liter, among the highest ever obtained.

K3 Magnette MG in two-place form of 1933. Author photo courtesy of the Briggs Cunningham Automotive Museum.

The small-engine racing classes in the '30s inspired a good deal of creative independent designs. One such design was the ERA, based out of the home and office of Raymond Mays. ERAs, like most others, were assembled from spare parts from existing production cars. Engines for ERAs were highly modified Riley sixes, for instance, with supercharging that developed 190 HP on alcohol.

ALFA ROMEO TIPO 158
1938

1.5-liter/90-CID twin-overhead-cam in-line 8-cylinder
w/single-stage blower
195 HP @ 7200 rpm
1367 lb, aluminum body on tubular frame
transverse-leaf swing-axle suspension

Suspension and chassis development lagged well behind engines, and handling sharp turns was a two-hand job, even for the refinements brought in the '30s. True, Dr. Porsche's Auto Union successfully introduced independent suspension, but it did not catch on. Also, changing gears in turns had always posed formidable problems. Because of a frequent need to shift gears at some critical point, or otherwise lose

power from dropping below the engine's torque band, a special transmission was developed. ERA and many other builders installed the Wilson preselector gearbox to free both hands for steering.

The Wilson was made by Armstrong-Siddeley in England and was an early-day "automatic" transmission. Drivers selected a gear before going into a turn. Depressing the clutch brought the next ratio (either up or down) into engagement which left both hands available for steering.

Such innovations helped drivers keep control of their cars. With their rigid axles, firm semi-elliptic springs, friction shocks and skinny, high-pressure tires, racing the cars meant spectacular four-wheel drifts through turns. Consequently, drivers were bounced and beaten around. In those days, racing was a great spectacle where driver skill was clearly visible in open cockpits.

In voiturette form, the K3 Magnette of 1934 was a single-seat entry from MG that posed the same sort of problems and sought the same sort of solutions. MG had been building sports and touring cars from 1922 when Cecil Kimber of Morris Garages thought he could make more money by selling sporting bodies on Morris Motors cars than their popular "Bullnose." His Oxford-based cars sold very well and launched MG as a marque.

MG left an illustrious legacy in the history of motor racing. Major international success followed the K3 Magnettes which were conceived as 1100cc international Class G cars between the 847cc Midgets and 1250cc Magnas. The K3 single-seaters were beautiful cars, low and rakish, rather like the Indy cars of the '50s. Their engines were SOHC supercharged in-line 1087cc sixes with a cross-flow head. In two-seat form, the cars followed the lines made so famous by MG.

Built for the 1933 Mille Miglia, the first K3 two-seat sports car went first into the Monte Carlo Rally where it performed with distinction. It and the second K3 built were then sent to Italy where the K3s simply slaughtered the stunned twin-cam Maserati opposition to win their class in the Mille Miglia. With that victory, MG was the first foreign marque to

33

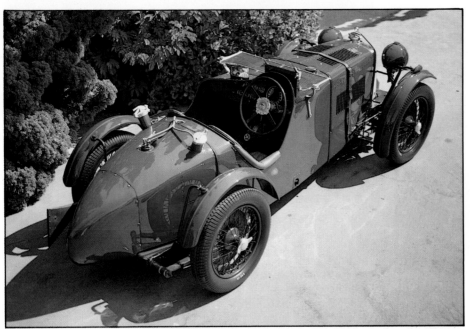

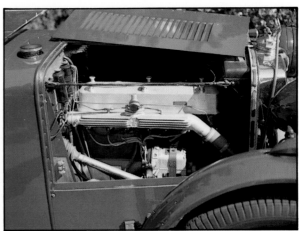

Cecil Kimber's MG works produced this overhead-cam in-line six-cylinder as an 1087cc engine between the 847cc Midget and the 1250cc Magna. With a bore and stroke of 57 X 71cc, output was 125 HP at 5500 rpm.

British Racing Green MGs gave a healthy surprise to their Italian competitors when the K3 team beat the twin-cam Maserati opposition to win the team prize in the Mille Miglia of 1933, the first non-Italian marque to do so. Author photo courtesy of the Briggs Cunningham Automotive Museum.

take the team prize in Italy's famous enduro. They then beat the single-seat Maseratis in the Coppo Acerbo Junior at Pescara. This victory attracted Nuvolari over to MG's camp, who later drove a K3 to win the RAC Tourist Trophy after breaking the class lap record seven times!

Amid all the glory and international recognition for MG, tragedy struck. Kaye Don overturned his K3 while testing and his passenger, an MG technician, was killed. The bad publicity that followed coincided with MG being sold to Morris Motors, who closed down Kimber's racing department.

Kimber had created MG and made the marque world famous, but the new management saw MG going in a different direction. During the war he was fired by the new management because he independently secured an aircraft contract for MG when top management planned armament production. So much for success.

MG K3 MAGNETTE
1933

1.1-liter/68-CID supercharged overhead-cam in-line 6-cylinder
125 HP @ 5500 rpm
aluminum body on ladder frame, leaf-spring suspension

Although open-wheel voiturettes received a lot of attention in racing, it was sports cars that captured the attention of the sporting buyer. Low-slung roadsters such as the MG offered buyers lots of fun for their money. The age of sports cars had begun.

ALLARD

The J-2X Allard. These British-built, American-powered cars were a handful, but virtually dominated club racing in America and Britain in the late '40s and early '50s. Allards were fitted with a variety of V8s that provided thrilling "basso profundo" sounds of big cubes.

Brooklands was the mecca of most British racing buffs early in this century. One of those chaps was Sydney Allard, who raced there in 1929 at the age of 19. With continued interest in racing in later years, he crossed different designs and ideas to create a marque of his own. The cars were understandably called Allards, and Syd's interesting approach was more American than British.

In 1930, his father bought him a Ford dealership in London. From that association came a sports-racing car that terrorized race tracks all around Britain. The first Allard was derived from a wrecked '34 Ford V8 fitted with Bugatti steering and bodywork. Chassis engineer Leslie Bellamy designed the curious split front axle that Allards became known for. The axle started life as a standard Ford I-beam type, split in the middle and pivoted there to allow the front wheels to operate independently.

Although not a conventional independent front suspension, it did provide some handling advantages over solid-axle front ends. Unfortunately, this was coupled with some very unusual characteristics—high roll center, unpredictable transient response and excessive camber and toe change with wheel travel. We know this latter phenomenon today as *bump steer*.

Although Allard's first car looked homemade, it was a huge success and became the foundation of production cars starting in 1946. Some specials were built, one with a Lincoln Zephyr V12, but Allard intended to offer a line of cars based on Ford power trains. Although several types were built, including a sedan with which Syd won the Monte Carlo rally in 1952, his aluminum-bodied J-series two-seat roadsters are of particular interest.

First of the J series was the J1. Its flathead Ford V8 gave exhilarating performance. It was replaced by the immortal J2 in 1949. The J2s could be built with one of several engines. One option was a Ford or Mercury

Most Allards were powered by overhead-valve Cadillacs and were known in their day as Cad-Allards. This is a rare Oldsmobile V8 fitted with Hilborn fuel injection.

With styling like many prewar cars, the Allard offered simple functionality, and a big steering wheel to hold on to. You needed it!

flathead V8 with Ardun conversion, delivering 140 HP as modified by Zora Arkus-Duntov. The conversion included aluminum cylinder heads with hemispherical combustion chambers.

The typical Allard J2 received a stock ohv Cadillac or Chrysler Hemi V8, both rated at more than 190 HP. As much as 300 HP was available from these engines with tuning and other minor modifications. Other engines could be fitted to the J2. Two built with Oldsmobile engines are known to exist today. One Olds-Allard won Sebring's over 5-liter class in 1954 with the Gray/Hall team averaging 61.1 mph for the 12 hours.

ALLARD J-2X
1952

5420cc/331-CID OHV Oldsmobile or Cadillac V8
w/single 4-bbl carb
up to 300 HP @ 4500 rpm
3-speed transmission, 2450 lb, aluminum body w/box steel frame
split-axle coil-spring independent front suspension
de Dion coil-spring rear suspension

The J2 Allards offered some chassis improvements over earlier models, such as front coil springs rather than leafs, but the split front axle was retained. The rear received a DeDion axle with coil springs, the first production British sports car so equipped.

With an abundance of power and torque, the J2 developed a reputation for being a fire-breathing, hair-chested beast that could lay waste to anything—if you could hang on! They could be slung around at will or sailed through the air, slid sideways anywhere and still roar off under massive acceleration.

Sydney Allard won the 1949 British Hillclimb Championship in his awesome car, then an Allard won the first U. S. Grand Prix at Watkins Glen.

In the 1950 running of the 24-Hours of LeMans, 26 different makes were among the 60 starters. A single Allard was entered and driven by its builder and Tom Cole to a third-place overall finish behind the Talbot-Lago GP cars in the first two positions. The Allard completed 2105.85 miles at an average speed of 87.74 mph, less than 2 mph off the pace of Rosier's winning Talbot.

In the Allard's waning days, Carroll Shelby and Sydney finished 10th overall in the 1000 Km of Buenos Aires of 1954 in a Cadillac Allard, and in 1956 the Bruno/Bruno team finished ninth overall.

J2 Allards were not small cars, nor were they light at some 2800 pounds. Then in 1951 came the J2-X, X for extended, with a 7.5-in. forward shift of the engine. Handling was said to be improved, no longer terrifying, just frightful. However, it continued to provide tense moments at the wheel. It was a brave man indeed who handled the cars for the 24 Hours of LeMans, as did Allard, Duntov and other drivers.

These British-built, aluminum-bodied hotrods represented the first serious use of American engines in production sport cars. The idea of engine swaps, long considered the southern California hotrodder's art, was well represented by Sydney's Allards. Allards were loud, exciting, strong and durable but were surpassed in the early '50s by cars from Ferrari, Jaguar and other builders who brought out better suspensions in lighter cars with equivalent power. Nevertheless, these hybrids wrote an interesting chapter of racing that is still alive today.

JAGUAR

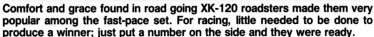
Comfort and grace found in road going XK-120 roadsters made them very popular among the fast-pace set. For racing, little needed to be done to produce a winner; just put a number on the side and they were ready.

The marque of the leaping Jaguar emerged as Britain's premier post-war sports car in 1948 with the introduction of the XK-120 and its superb twin-cam, in-line six-cylinder engine. XK-120 coachwork showed some BMW 328 Mille Miglia influence. The engine was a technical masterpiece.

That six-cylinder would require a well-deserved volume to recount its contributions to the world of sports cars. But more important is Jaguar's emergence as a leading sports car, as proven in competition.

The engine originated during lengthy hours of fire watching as Hitler attempted to annihilate Britain. A group of Jaguar engineers sat about discussing the future, and batted around ideas. One central to their discussions was the possibility of building a twin overhead-cam passenger-car engine, an unheard of task.

Prewar SS Jaguars, most notably the SS-100, gave Sir William

Lyons a measure of success. Building on such heritage, Lyons renamed his company Jaguar Cars Ltd. The SS initials held sinister overtones of Nazi Germany, but actually stood for *Standard Swallow*. Because Lyons had developed sizable exports before the war, British officials allowed Jaguar to secure sufficient quantities of steel to mount a renewed export drive. The national decree was to export manufactured goods to get material to produce, and America was an excellent market.

Lyons insisted that the new engine not only perform and be durable, but also look good. The symmetry of the twin overhead-cam design was complemented by a polished cast-aluminum cam-drive and cam cover. Technical advantages of the overhead-cam design were obvious—hemispherical combustion chambers, crossflow manifolding and a lightweight, high-speed valve train—and held huge potential for performance, especially when compared to the prevailing pushrod, six-cylinder Jaguar power plant. But the project was certainly a bold undertaking and costly considering there was no assurance of market acceptance.

From today's perspective, the XK-120 twin-cam six was a stroke of brilliance, a superlative contribution to automobiles and certainly one of Britain's foremost engines. It has been the heart of thousands of Jaguars.

The engine, as first offered, was a 160-HP, 3442cc unit that propelled the car at speeds of 120 mph—hence the name. The car was magnificent with flowing proportions. But the Jaguar was not a static piece to be admired. It was a sports car whose dynamics were meant to be enjoyed. And it was a trendsetter that caught most other builders completely by surprise.

William Lyons insisted on a twin-cam engine for his new sports car. With a bore and stroke of 83 X 106mm displacing 3442cc and a compression ratio of up to 9:1, 180 HP at 5300 rpm was achievable with optional equipment.

JAGUAR XK-120
1951

3442 cc/210-CID DOHC 6-cylinder
160 HP @ 5300 rpm
4-speed transmission, 3015 lb, steel body and frame
independent front suspension, leaf-spring rear suspension

Initially an experiment, only 240 XK-120s were built to test the market, but demand was overwhelming. The new Jags were cars of character. Final production tallied over 12,000!

The XK-120 also showed that Jaguar could carry Britain's colors on the world's race tracks and proceeded to put the needle of second best to many other marques. Luigi Chinetti had given Italy's new marque, Ferrari, a rousing start with all sorts of wins, including LeMans 1949. But it was Jaguar that showed six-cylinder power in well-rounded cars to be often superior to robust V12s.

Production XK-120 Jaguars left the Foleshill Works in July 1949. Their first competition was in the Silverstone Production Car Race in August. It was Britain's first big race since the war, and the two XK-120s entered left the field well behind. With that beginning, Jaguars were entered at LeMans 1950 where Talbot-Lagos, really GP cars with lights and fenders, won with a 1-2 finish. Leslie Johnson, winner of the Silverstone race, moved his Jaguar into third position before failing brakes sidelined the car. Even so, Jaguar's LeMans performance was an impressive showing against many specialized cars. It launched Jaguar into international racing. From such stirring of the spirit, a special competition Jaguar for LeMans was conceived—the C-type.

The aim was to win LeMans 1951, and Jaguar engineers set about the task with dedication. They had six months to design, build and develop the car. Although called the XK-120C, the car they produced was very different from the XK-120. It received a new tubular chassis, a lightweight aluminum body with a flip-up front section, and a new torsion-bar rear suspension to replace the existing leaf-spring setup. Engine power increased to 210 HP with a high-compression cylinder head, bigger carburetors and an improved exhaust system.

To solve the brake problem, Jaguar undertook another bold maneuver that later became a major contribution to automotive development. Brakes were a major point of failure for many cars in the post-

C-type Jaguar glory was first won at LeMans 1951, where the Walker/Whitehead team was victorious and Stirling Moss set the fastest lap, 105.532 mph. C-types won again in 1953 with a spectacular 1-2 finish.

CUNNINGHAM

The Cunningham C-4R, one of America's greatest sports/racing cars. This is the Sebring winner of 1953. Driven by Phil Walters and John Fitch, this Chrysler Hemi powered car posted its win with an average of 74.9 mph in Sebring's first FIA sanctioned 12-hour endurance race. The Spear/Johnston team drove this C-4R to 3rd at LeMans, 1954.

For the 1953 season, FIA initiated the World Manufacturer's Championship for sports cars. Interest in such racing spread throughout Europe and America and spawned all sorts of cars, both racing and production. Some were to become legends, Jaguar, Porsche and Ferrari for instance, while others were competitive but didn't succeed in the marketplace.

Jaguar never won the manufacturer's championship because the company never really tried. Ferrari went after the title feverishly, and Aston Martin always seemed to be in the fight. American entrants in European-style racing have always been few. But during the early '50s, American sportsman, Briggs S. Cunningham, launched a line of cars that were competitive. The cars that bore his name showed signs of being another great marque, but slipped into obscurity after a short, but brilliant, racing career.

His firm, Cunningham Cars Ltd., was not able to show a profit within five years, and that was the law from the Internal Revenue Service. In the eyes of the revenuers, Cunningham was not a business, only a hobby without tax breaks.

Briggs S. Cunningham, S. as in the Swift Foods fortune, was well steeped in sports cars from his early Automobile Racing Club of America—ARCA—racing days with the Colliers in Florida. He believed that Americans could challenge anyone from anywhere in any sport and win. Cunningham proved the point in yachting, among other sports, then undertook to make America's international racing colors of white and blue a LeMans winner.

His interest in racing machines was to produce all-American cars to beat the Europeans on their own turf, LeMans in particular. He very nearly succeeded, but a little behind-the-scenes politics stopped him.

Florida was a hotbed of American sports-car racing after World War II. The flat airport course in the central Florida town of Sebring had emerged as the place to race. As the only World Manufacturer's Championship circuit in the United States, Sebring drew the best cars and teams in the world. Cunningham established his business in West Palm Beach, Florida.

A string of victories in 1953—54 makes this Cunningham C-4R a true legend of American racing. The oil cooler on the left of the cowl is a Cunningham trait that added life to its 331-CID, 325-HP Chrysler Hemi engine.

At 5.4-liters displacement, the Chrysler Hemi placed the C4-R in the 8-liter class of international racing where they reigned supreme at LeMans, 1951—54. Compared to the Allard that won the 8-liter class in 1950, 2105.853 miles at an average speed of 87.74 mph, this C-4R completed 2367.38 miles in 24 hours at a race average of 98.64 mph.

56

In 1949, Cunningham met Phil Walters and Bill Frick who were building their *Fordillacs*—Fords with Cadillac engines. His proposal to field cars at LeMans was well received by Frick and Walters. But, because there was no "manufacturer" of the Fordillacs—they were not *homologated*—LeMans officials would not accept their entry. From their experience with Cadillac engines and the desire to gain LeMans experience, Cunningham and his team entered two other cars in the 24-Hours of 1950.

CUNNINGHAM C-4R
1953

5424cc/331-CID OHV Chrysler Hemi V8 w/4 carbs
325 HP @ 5000 rpm
4-speed transmission, aluminum body w/tubular steel frame
independent coil-spring front suspension
Chrysler live rear axle w/coil springs

One was a basically stock Cadillac Coupe de Ville while the second was a special-bodied Caddy streamliner dubbed "Le Monstre" by disbelieving Frenchmen. So, the new American challenge began with Cadillacs, no less. During the race, Briggs stuffed "Le Monstre" into a sand

bank and lost time getting back on the track. Water leaks and transmission problems prevented the Coupe de Ville from finishing higher than 10th. "Le Monstre" was faster on the Mulsanne Straight at 134 mph, but finished 11th due to its earlier altercation. The purpose of the exercise was to finish, and that they did while proving the worth of American V8 engines.

A new Cunningham works was set up in 1951 for the purpose of building and campaigning racing cars. The first was the Cunningham C-1 with rather European styling and Cadillac power. Although a road car rather than a racing machine, the car was well received by the press. It established Cunningham as a marque.

Next came the C-2R, a purpose-built racing car offered initially with either a Cadillac or the new Chrysler Hemi engine. However, only the Hemi saw production, and Chrysler engineering performed extensive engine development for Cunningham. Reportedly, the C-2R was clocked at 152 mph in tests and showed that Briggs was on the "right track" for LeMans.

In the 1951 24-Hours, Walters and Fitch ran as high as second behind the eventual winner, the C-type Jag, and finished 18th overall to take the 8-liter class. Lessons learned brought about the C-3R, but the decision was made to offer this new Cunningham as a Grand Touring car and to develop yet another racer. Thus, the C-4R—a resounding success that became one of America's all-time winningest sports racers.

With its four-carb, 325-HP Hemi engine, four-speed transmission, short-wheelbase, lightweight-alloy body and smaller overall design, the C-4R looked every bit the LeMans challenger it was intended to be. Two roadsters and a coupe were built and entered at LeMans, 1952. Cunningham and former rival, Bill Spear, teamed to a fourth-place overall finish and won the 8-liter class. This was the second class win for Cunningham's cars, and bettered the class distance record set two years earlier by an Allard, also an American V8-powered racer.

A C-4R won overall at Sebring and led both an Aston Martin (second) and a C-Jag (third) at the finish. Fitch and Walters completed 173 laps, 28 more laps than the 1952 winner, a Frazer-Nash with 145 laps. The Aston Martin finished one lap down.

The C-4Rs were highly competitive, but the big news was the C-5R of 1953. It shot the Mulsanne Straight at LeMans at 156 mph and took a third overall to break Jaguar's hoped for 1-2-3 sweep with their disc-brake-equipped C-types. The 1953 LeMans was the first to see cars average more than 100 mph, and the C-5R clocked a race average of 104.09 mph, just 1.8 mph off the 105.84-mph winning pace of Rolt and Hamilton's Jag.

Cunningham noted the advantages of disc brakes and placed an order with Dunlop for his 1954 cars. As the LeMans race date drew near, Dunlop sent a notice that his order could not be placed until a date after the 24-Hour duel. Europeans had long dominated their premier race, and such preventive politics showed that the continentals meant to keep it that way. The Cunninghams ran anyway, with the Spear/Johnston team taking third overall and the 8-liter class win again with their 5.4-liter C-4R. The Cunningham/Bennet C-4R was fifth.

New engine regulations ruled out the V8 Cunninghams for 1955, and even though a C-6R with an Indy-type Offenhauser ran, it was not up to the rigors of endurance racing.

1955 saw the last of the Cunningham cars, but not Briggs Cunningham. The IRS equated his firm's heavy financial losses and no profits to a hobby, an expensive one no doubt, and refused to allow the benefits of business taxation. Briggs continued racing with considerable success,

The Spear/Johnston team drove to a third overall at LeMans, 1954 in this cockpit. An American-designed and -built, American-powered and -driven racing car, this C-4R Cunningham was the last American car to finish high at LeMans until 1960 when a Corvette finished eighth.

but mostly in European cars.

America's blue and white racing colors were seen on Jaguars, OSCAs, Ferraris and other European marques from Cunningham's team, as well as later Corvettes. The IRS saw to it that only major manufacturers could go into racing with any chance of winning.

MASERATI A6GCS

58

Best known today as the Koster Maserati, this one-off roadster was built to Fritz Koster's specifications and is the last Maserati built with the classic double-oval grille. It is one of the first postwar Masers with a twin-overhead-cam engine—this one with an aluminum block unlike earlier cast-iron versions. Ewing Hunter photo.

Spartan in the Italian style of the early '50s, A6GCS coachwork shows the car to be small and mainly of aluminum construction. The large wood-rimmed wheel is characteristic of the time. Ewing Hunter photo.

Big American V8s in lightweight cars were top racing competitors in the late 1940s and early '50s. Allard-Ferrari battles became popular after Scuderia Ferrari introduced its 4.2-liter cars for the purpose of going head-to-head with Sydney Allard's cars.

Along with those shootouts were the huge successes of Jaguar XK-120s and their record runs in Europe (132.6-mph flying mile, Jabbeke, Belgium, 1949) that brought about factory advertising such as, "The fastest production sports car in the world." The acclaim of the famous trident waned in the late '40s, and a new model was needed to regain the good name of Maserati in racing.

Sports-car racing in America and Europe was reaching new highs, and Maserati jumped into the fray with its first postwar model, the six-cylinder A6GC-2000, better known as the *A6GCS*. Advertisements of 1952 listed the heavily louvered car as a contender for the newly established Formula 2 class of international competition. Its double overhead-cam (DOHC) engine displaced 1988cc and produced 145 HP at

7000 rpm. Top speed was claimed to be 150 mph. About 10 A6GCS Maseratis were built.

The new Maserati doubled as a sports-racing two-seater whose fenders could be removed for F-2 racing. Its origin dated from the A6 built in 1941, then rebodied by Pinin Farina in the spring of '47.

It was also in 1947 that the Maserati brothers' contract with the Orsi family of Modena expired. Aldolfo and Omer Orsi had purchased the Maserati firm from the brothers in 1937. Under terms of the contract, the services of the Maserati brothers were retained for a decade. In 1947, the brothers were free to return to building their own cars, but could not use the Maserati name. It was retained under the Orsi contract. They returned to Bologna to build OSCA cars, page 65.

The Maserati designation, *GCS*, translated into *G*, ghisa or cast-iron engine block, and *CS*, as corsa sport or sports-racing model. The *G* was retained even for later cars in the series that received aluminum-alloy blocks.

Designed for the hotly contested 2-liter formula, the 1952—53 World Championship series, the Maserati DOHC six-cylinder engine was advertised at 145 HP at 7000 rpm with a top speed of 150 mph. In final form as shown, power tops 170 HP. Ewing Hunter photo.

MASERATI A6GCS
1953

1960cc/120-CID DOHC in-line 6-cylinder
165 HP @ 7000 rpm w/Weber carburetors
4-speed transmission
1628 lb, aluminum body w/tubular steel frame
coil-spring independent front suspension
leaf-spring independent rear suspension

The selection of a car that fit Formula 2 racing rules was fortuitous in that the series drew spirited competition on the continent. Formula 2 actually replaced Formula 1 in 1952 and '53. In that series, a private-entry team from Argentina, Equipe/Achille/Varzi, provided some interesting input when they installed an A6GCS engine in an earlier-design Maserati 4CLT/48 single-seat chassis. Juan Fangio scored a victory in such a car, and showed that the idea had merit.

The car's coil-spring and wishbone suspension gave excellent handling, and continual improvements brought the Maseratis up to Formula 2 potential. Heated battles between Ferrari and Maserati gave spectators many exhilarating moments. At the Grand Prix of Modena, a hometown crowd witnessed a photo finish that showed Maserati had the speed and power to run with Ferrari.

Changed sports-car racing rules for 1953 effectively outlawed cycle fenders. This brought about the quick-disconnect, removable fenders with quarter-turn fasteners on the last A6GCS chassis. This became a prototype Maserati sports car, the one referred to above. This car remained a one-off, although it was used in factory advertising and made available to the press. The car was sold to a Dutch racing driver, Fritz Koster, who had been the co-winner of the first Sebring race, a six-hour handicapper, in a 724cc Crosley.

Koster entered his Maser in other races, then sent it back to the Modena works for updating. Afterward, he entered the car in the Dutch GP of June 1953. With some driving pointers from Fangio, Koster was sufficiently inspired and sped off to a handsome lead in the LeMans start. Slowed later by failing brakes, Koster was passed by Cliff Davis's Tojeiro-Bristol.

Koster then returned to the United States for SCCA racing and firmly established himself and the car as an almost unbeatable team in their class. They frequently bested more powerful C-type Jags. Koster continually updated his Maserati roadster for improved performance and, in final form, extracted some 170 HP at 7500 rpm. This team also raced in a memorable battle against Huschke von Hanstein in a Porsche 550 spyder for fourth place at Nassau in 1954. Von Hanstein later became Porsche racing manager.

The 1625-pound car has survived in remarkable form and retains its twin-plug head, twin ignition, four-speed transmission, bolt-on fenders and charisma. It's the only Maserati of its kind, a small and exciting car that has participated in vintage racing for some two decades. Although not a product of the Maserati brothers, the Koster A6GCS is an interesting look at the first postwar Orsi Maserati.

TOJEIRO-ACE

Tojeiro-Ace prototype that laid the foundation of the AC Ace and AC Cobra roadsters. Britisher, John Tojeiro, built upon the ideas shown in Cooper cars and produced this independent-suspension two-seater.

The rebuilding of Britain's postwar economy sparked all sorts of automotive cottage industries. Interest in racing was widespread, but most manufacturers were concentrating on producing sedans—saloons—rather than sports cars. Thus, there was a ready market for sports cars and racing machines. It fostered a lot of automotive creativity. One such product was the work of a Cambridgeshire villager of Portuguese origin, John Tojeiro.

In the early '50s, Tojeiro raced a modified MG-TA, but thought performance could be improved with all-independent suspension. There were examples of such a design already proven in competition. Charles Cooper and his son John were building 500cc single-seaters with the ingredients Tojeiro was looking for: A twin-tube ladder-type frame with transverse leaf springs, front and rear, that sprung wishbones at each corner. Their Cooper-MG was a sports car of similar design with a Ferrari barchetta-inspired aluminum body.

Noted British driver, Cliff Davis, drove the Cooper-MG to victory numerous times including the prestigious Daily Express Rally, a 1250-mile trek around Britain. Wanting more power, he commissioned a second car to be built. Tojeiro got the job. Davis then secured the 140-HP Bristol in-line six. The same engine had been used by the Gilby Engineering Frazer-Nash that powered Stirling Moss to victory in the 1951 British Empire Trophy. The new Tojeiro car featured an unpainted aluminum body, the lines of which were reminiscent of the 166MM Ferrari barchetta. Their aluminum bodies were polished and displayed the famous registration numbers of JOY 500 and LOY 500 respectively.

On the Tojeiro-Bristol's first outing, Davis took the Easter running at Goodwood, then capped off a very impressive season with a victory in the Dutch Grand Prix at Zandvoort against the Koster Maserati. While Davis was racing, Vincent Davison of Tojeiro's employ completed another very similar car, but fitted it with a 2.5-liter, 100-HP Lea-Francis six obtained from Connaught. That firm was becoming increasingly involved in F-1 racing and less interested in their promising L3 sports model with a 1767cc Lea-Francis engine.

The new car was impressively demonstrated by Davis to Derek

Hurlock and E. H. Sidney of AC Cars, who were looking for a sports car for production. Legend has it that a deal was struck over lunch one day, and Davison went with the car to AC to help develop the stark sports/racer into a tourer.

In October 1953, AC Cars created a sensation at the Earls Court Motor Show with their version of the Tojeiro-Bristol, the AC Ace. It was the first production all-independently sprung British sports car. A legend was begun. The Ace line became a respected and successful series of cars, then formed the foundation for Carroll Shelby's famous AC Cobras of the '60s.

Instead of the Bristol engine, AC chose to offer the new Ace with its own less-powerful, overhead-cam 2-liter six. The car weighed around 1800 pounds and was fitted with AC's faithful four-speed Moss gearbox, synchronized in second, third and fourth gears. Dunlop 15-inch wire wheels replaced the Turner alloy wheels used by Davis.

The AC Ace prototype was tested by British journalist, John Bolton, who reported it to be an attractive, tractable 100-mph car with superb roadholding. Its AC 2-liter engine was a light-alloy block with a cast-iron head and a single chain-driven cam. Power was reported to be 85 HP at 4500 rpm from a 7.5:1 compression ratio. That was sufficient to post 0-60-mph times of 10.5 seconds. The car was well-mannered and gave no hint of its latent performance when driven conservatively.

This car was built by Vincent Davison of Tojeiro's firm and was demonstrated by Cliff Davis for officials of AC Cars, Ltd. They bought it and the AC Ace line of sports cars was shown first at Earls Court in 1953.

TOJEIRO-ACE PROTOTYPE
1953

2553cc/156-CID OHV in-line Ford Zephyr 6-cylinder in final form
170 HP @ 5800 rpm w/Weber carburetors
4-speed Moss transmission
1175 lb, aluminum body w/tubular steel frame
transverse-leaf independent front and rear suspension

Weight distribution neared the ideal with a 46/54% front/rear proportion, and brakes were drum-type Wellworthy Alfins with Morris Minor hubs. The final drive was a mounted ENV/Jaguar unit that drove Hardy Spicer articulated shafts. The Ace power train and suspension layout carried on through the AC Cobra that took the World Manufacturer's Championship from Ferrari in 1965—quite a tribute to Tojeiro's chassis design.

This first Ace prototype, registered TPL 792, was introduced to racing by Davis a few weeks after its introduction in the Daily Express Rally. With that beginning, the Ace line gathered many wins over its production lifetime. But the need for more power to remain competitive brought about the use of two other engines. One was a Bristol unit and the other a Ford Zephyr six.

Using the 100D2 Bristol engine was largely in response to Ken Rudd, an AC dealer, who recognized that realizing the Ace's potential against newer sports cars would require more power. This expensive hemispherical-combustion-chamber engine became available in 1956, and the Zephyr 2.6-liter came on line in 1961. Ken Rudd's famed "Rudd-

Typically British, like the preceding C-type Jaguar, the dash of the Tojeiro-Ace was spartan with only the barest of essentials. John Bolton proclaimed it an attractive, tractable 100-mph car with superb roadholding.

speed Ace" cars were pure performance machines fitted with Weber carburetors and delivering 155 HP.

Final production breakdown by engine was 226 with the AC engine, 465 with the 1971cc Bristol engine developing 125 HP and 36 with the Ford Zephyr unit. The Tojeiro-Ace is a fine example of Britain's automobile cottage industry of the early 1950s, and of the work of a few dedicated men developing sports cars with superb potential.

MG "T" CARS

MG-TDs pitting after storming along Mid-Ohio's twisty sports-car course.

High-speed bump control was one race-car virtue that came relatively late in chassis development. Independent suspensions had clearly shown their advantages over earlier types, and by the mid-'50s, most motorsport enthusiasts regarded prewar chassis as antiquated. So why was the MG-TC such a popular car?

The car looked prewar, and many MG fans regarded the TC as little more than its immediate prewar predecessor, the MG-TB. Some considered the even earlier PB a superior car.

What endeared the TC in the hearts of most Americans was its availability at a particular time. We've seen that Britain's economy was very shaky after the war, albeit better than most other European countries. America emerged strong with three times its prewar industrial capacity. The end of the austere days of rationing and saving were impatiently awaited. In short, the typical American worker was burdened with cash and pent-up desire for consumer goods not produced during wartime, especially cars.

The wait for desirable new models was so great that it took auto manufacturers three years to catch up with demand. American servicemen in Britain received handsome American wages, and because the MG-TC was the only sports car available in quantity, they bought them and took them home to America. The year was 1947 and nothing like the TC was being built by U.S. manufacturers.

It was in this climate that the MG-TC became part of the American scene—a very affectionate part. Some historians claim the MG to be the car that brought sports-car fever to America. Fun-seeking young buyers made the MG into a favorite. The car was in the right place at the right time at the right price. And it was fun.

The MG-TC exemplified the wind-in-the-face sports-car experience—pure joie de vivre. It was highly admired despite its prewar technical virtues. Archaic in design and construction with poor bump control, the MG-TC nevertheless became a classic. It's still regarded as one of the most desirable postwar British cars.

This 1949 MG-TC strikes the form of days of old. They are the cars that brought thrilling driving to America following the second war. Their prewar lines have long been a recognized classic.

This 1954 MG-TF shows the final development of the "T" series before the introduction of the MGA.

The TC also helped create the self-image of a true sports-car enthusiast some still accept. It was of no concern that his car was leaky, drafty, noisy, harsh riding, cold, cramped, temperamental and looked old-fashioned. He was the sophisticated and dashing, devil-may-care sportsman of continental taste who forsook comforts for the sheer pleasure of driving. The MG-TC was his medium.

In a new age of advanced materials in auto construction, the TC had oak bracing in the doors and oak framing in the body. The fire wall was separated from the cowling by more wood. Even the floorboards were just that—plywood!

But then, what other cars were its contemporaries? Compared to the likes of wallowing and bulbous American sedans and convertibles, land barges of disgustingly little excitement, the TC was a graceful thing of beauty. Its 1930s-like lines were classic and a breath of fresh air. With the revival of SCCA motorsports, the MG played a prominent role in the emergence of many American race-car drivers.

Briggs Cunningham campaigned a supercharged TC, and Fred Wacker, SCCA competitor and later pensman, became a TC star. Another TC driver, John Fitch, became one of few Americans to successfully race in European events. Then there was Phil Hill, who claims the TC changed his whole life. He became World Champion.

As with Florida and New England, California was abuzz with sports-car-racing fever. Western U.S. racing of the early '50s usually consisted of two main events, one for modified cars under 1500cc and another for modifieds over 1500cc. Early on, Roger Barlow's Simca

specials were dominant in the smaller class. Next were the 1342cc OSCAs, followed by Porsche Spyders that cleaned house.

In 1953, Ken Miles, who was service manager for a southern California MG distributor, went racing with his homebuilt, cycle-fendered MG special, dubbed the R1. Later to become a legend, the thin Englishman entered his MG special in the under-1500 class at Pebble Beach that year and produced a splendid victory. The next year, Miles and his R1 beat everything and everybody in his class. Miles usually ran

MG-TF 1500
1955

1466cc/90-CID in-line OHV 4-cylinder
63 HP @ 5500 rpm
4-speed transmission, 2010 lb, steel body w/box steel frame
coil-spring independent front suspension,
leaf-spring rear suspension

in the over-1500 class as well, and frequently laid waste to bigger cars. In their ten main-event starts, Miles and his R1 was never beaten, even against the dreaded OSCAs.

The R1's flywheel bolts sheared at Pebble Beach 1954 while leading, putting Miles out of the race. Thus sidelined, Miles sold the R1 to

"T" series MGs have long been a great favorite. They began the racing careers of many top drivers and promoted the MG "Safety Fast" image.

build another special-bodied car. The R2, affectionately called the *Flying Shingle* because it looked like one, continued where the R1 left off. It established Miles and MG firmly in California racing. Miles became a folk hero among many competitors, most of whom broke their MGs racing against OSCAs and Porsches. Miles succeeded in putting the Italian and German cars in their place, much to the pleasure of his fellow MG racers. He was regarded as the best there was.

European MG fans were no less affectionate for the cars and teams. The prewar Cream Crackers and Musketeers have already been mentioned, but after the war the new management at Abingdon held no interest in competition. Although the factory had no association with the car, a privately held special set a new class record of 159.15 mph in 1946 and showed that an MG could be quite fast indeed. The car went on to set a string of remarkable records while running on three cylinders.

With the MG Works riding on healthy profits, there was little incentive to support a competition effort. But a management shuffle in 1947 brought in people less opposed to racing. TC sales climbed from 1700 in 1946 to 5000 in 1949 and over 10,000 in 1950. With increasing demand, a new project was undertaken to produce an improved car. The TD was introduced in 1949. A team of three rather standard TDs took the first three places in class and the team prize in the Tourist Trophy that year.

In 1952, MG merged with Austin, Britain's other major builder, to become the British Motor Corp. Another new MG was being prepared, but the new BMC top management reached an agreement to produce Donald Healey's new Healey 100 before being shown the new MG. Healey's car was based on Austin components and was a fortuitous means of using up a stockpile of Austin parts. Thus, the new MG was shelved and sales began to slip to the Healey and Triumph TR2.

In an attempt to hold on to sales, the TD was given a face lift to make it lower and sleeker. It was also fitted with a larger, more powerful engine. This became the TF (the TE designation was bypassed), introduced in October 1953. It was the last of the T series MGs. Many now regard it as the prettiest of the "classic" MGs. George Phillips' sleek LeMans MG of 1951 inspired the MGA introduced to racing in 1955.

O.S.C.A.

(Above) OSCA, the second generation product from the Maserati brothers. MT-4 sports/racing cars like this one were the terror of small-engine class racing. Author photo courtesy of the Briggs Cunningham Automotive Museum.

(Right) Magnificent, yet functional OSCA styling is shown in the smooth contours that competitors came to fear. Like other styles of the time, these sports cars had character that became lost in the age of aerodynamics. Author photo courtesy of the Briggs Cunningham Automotive Museum.

The Brothers Maserati formed their company in 1926 and soon established themselves as builders of respected Grand Prix cars. From their Bologna, Italy, shop came high-quality cars that set high standards as fast, reliable racers.

The general decline of industry in Italy in the '30s and the emergence of the overwhelming German GP cars forced the sale of the Maserati company in 1937. Its new owners, Adolfo and Omer Orsi, moved the works to Modena. The terms of the sale retained the services of Ernesto, Bindo and Ettore Maserati for 10 years. Upon the agreement's expiration in 1947, the brothers returned to Bologna. There they established a firm specializing in building racing cars, but the Orsi agreement did not allow the brothers to use their own name.

They formed a new company, Officina Specializzata Costruzioni Automobille - Fratelli Maserati (O.S.C.A.), and undertook the development of an engine for the second formula of the then current Formula-1 rules. Instead of a supercharged 1.5-liter engine, their's was an unblown 4.5-liter V12 with single overhead cams and two valves per cylinder.

Among OSCA's first efforts were 1.1-liter sports/racing roadsters.

Power was by a Fiat block fitted with a high-performance single overhead-cam head, backed by a four-speed transmission. The new cars were built on a tubular frame with a coil spring-and-wishbone front suspension and a rigid axle and quarter-elliptics at the rear. Later OSCAs received independent rear suspension. These cars were designated MT-4 for Maserati-Type four cylinder. Larger-displacement versions were built later.

The new OSCA design scored a clear victory in its second outing, the Grand Prix of Naples. Luigi Villoresi, two-time Targa Florio winner (in a Maserati), won over a Ferrari driven by two-time LeMans winner Raymond Sommer (with Chinetti in '32 and Nuvolari in '33 in Alfas), and a Maserati driven by Alberto Ascari, who would become World Driving Champion in 1952 and '53.

Other minor victories followed. Then came the Mille Miglia of 1950, a great showing for Luigi Fagioli, who won class honors in a 1.1-liter OSCA over previous class victors. For more power, Ernesto Maserati produced an in-house twin-cam engine to replace the Fiat based four-cylinder. The new powerplant made OSCA the terror of the

Later OSCA MT-4 in full race trim shows forward-pivoting front end and faired-in headrest for driver.

The OSCA four-cylinder, twin-overhead-cam engine: In the MT-4, this little engine was a jewel of performance and reliability. This 1452cc OSCA engine powered Bill Lloyd and Stirling Moss to victory in 1954 at an average speed of 73.6 mph for the 12 Hour. Author photo courtesy of the Briggs Cunningham Automotive Museum.

OSCA MT-4
1954

1453cc/89-CID DOHC in-line 4-cylinder
110 HP @ 7000 rpm
4-speed transmission, aluminum body w/tubular frame
coil-spring independent front suspension
live rear axle w/quarter elliptic leafs

small-engine class in both Europe and America.

Perhaps OSCA's most impressive Italian race was the Targa Florio of 1956. That race was riddled with bad luck for the big cars, allowing Umberto Maglioli a spectacular finish in a tough, but small, 550 Porsche. In the confusion following the LeMans 1955 disaster, in which scores of spectators were killed, the CSI rules committee had wanted the Targa shortened and only one driver per car. Vincenzo Florio hotly contested that ruling and forced a last-minute change back to 10 laps around the 44.6-mile Piccolo Madonie circuit of Sicily, versus the proposed eight, and reinstated two drivers. Then, in a mix-up, von Hanstein's name was left off the Porsche driver list, so Maglioli drove the entire race himself. His win was all the more spectacular, being a solo drive.

The OSCA of Cabianca and Villoresi stuck close to the Porsche during the final laps and finished a very impressive second overall. To have two small cars victorious was an embarrassment for both Ferrari and Maserati, especially at the hands of the German Porsche. OSCA salvaged some Italian pride but to no avail.

A protest over a technicality concerning the OSCA's official driver entrants resulted in the car being disqualified. Its glorious finish was struck from the record and the battered Maserati of Pierro Taruffi was awarded second place. The horribly battered Ferrari of Olivier Gendebien and Hans Herrmann came in third.

OSCAs were brought to the United States and raced widely. The 12-Hour of 1953 was Sebring's first year as an official FIA race in the World Manufacturer's Championship series. It was also America's only race with that distinction, and Briggs Cunningham entered an OSCA in which he and Bill Lloyd drove to seventh overall by completing 151 out of 173 laps turned in by Cunningham's own winning C-4R. Another OSCA finished ninth.

The year 1954 was to see a major win for OSCA at Sebring. With its international stature, the 12-Hour that year drew several factory teams. One was Lancia with four cars to battle Jaguar, Ferrari, Cunningham and other top teams. As expected, the Lancias dominated the early stages but didn't have the endurance to win.

Stirling Moss and Bill Lloyd in Cunningham's OSCA started 14th and steadily worked their way up in the field. Taruffi's Lancia held a big lead, but its engine seized, letting the OSCA take the lead and the win ahead of another Lancia that was three laps back. Three other OSCAs finished in fourth, fifth and eighth positions. As a 1452cc car, the Moss/Lloyd OSCA also took the Index of Performance making an OSCA clean sweep.

A variety of OSCAs was built through 1963 with engines from 750cc to 1600cc in racing and GT form. The Brothers Maserati sold their works that year to Count Agusta, manufacturer of the MV Agusta motorcycles. That brought about the end of the giant-killer OSCAs, except for those few that are vintage-raced today.

FOUR CYLINDER FERRARIS

The Pinin Farina-bodied 500 Mondial is an example of Scuderia Ferrari's brief encounter with four cylinders. This was the sports-car version of the single-seat 2-liter Monza driven by Ascari to the World Championship in 1952—53.

Enzo Ferrari apparently sought to provide winning cars in all sorts of classes. His V12s had already established the marque, but 12 cylinders were thirsty and in shorter races, pit stops were costly. Thus, smaller engines had the advantage of more modest fuel consumption.

Another aspect contributing to the rise of four-cylinder Ferraris was FIA's rule change. For 1952 and '53, the world championship was based on 2-liter Formula-2 cars rather than Formula-1s. Ferrari's engine man, Aurelio Lampredi, had already been working on two four-cylinder engines. The foundation was laid for Ferrari's first experimental four-banger sports car. It was completed in 1953.

The weight savings over the V12 was almost 100 pounds, and with four cylinders, the engine had about half the moving parts. Lampredi's initial analysis indicated that the power-to-weight ratio of a four cylinder could be 12—15 percent better than the V12. He was vindicated when the first such engine, built in the spring of 1951, turned out 170 HP versus 155 of the V12. That was a 28% improvement in power-to-weight ratio;

specific output was also improved. The new engine delivered 85.9 HP/liter versus 77.8 HP/liter for the V12, almost 10% better.

The new 2-liter engine powered Ferrari and Alberto Ascari to the 1952—53 Manufacturer's and Driver's World Championship with 11 wins out of 15 starts. The engine then became the foundation for the new 500 Mondial sports car. A subsequent four-cylinder engine producing 180 HP at 7000 rpm went into the first Testa Rossa.

The Mondial engine was a twin-plug, DOHC design with two valves per cylinder inclined at 60°. Two Marelli magnetos were used. Carburetion was by two sidedraft Webers. Carburetor-throat size could be changed to vary peak output and bottom-end response.

Generally speaking, the 500 Mondial was a sports-car version of Ascari's single-seat 2-liter Monza. Bodies were first built by Pinin Farina and later by Scaglietti. Some 34 of the 500 Mondials were built, no two exactly alike.

Frames were welded tubular steel. Farina bodies featured an independent front suspension of unequal-length A-arms sprung by a transverse leaf spring. Scaglietti-bodied cars had coil springs instead of leafs.

The Lampredi-designed four-cylinder Mondial engine, successor to the elegant little 2-liter V12 of Colombo. These 5-main-bearing engines were 92 lb lighter and produced 15 more HP in first form. Later versions at 180 HP became the Testa Rossa. Still later, the engine was taken to a full 3 liters and produced 250 HP in the 750 Monza.

By the time the 500 Mondial was introduced in 1953, 35 previous Ferraris had been produced beginning with the 125GT of 1946. Once the Cunningham and J-2 Allard threat had been laid to rest, SCCA racing became all Ferrari. Top American drivers, Phil Hill, Dan Gurney, Richie Ginther, Carroll Shelby and Masten Gregory learned much of their skill in cockpits like this.

FERRARI 500 MONDIAL
1954

1985cc/121-CID DOHC in-line 4-cylinder w/twin-plug head
170 HP @ 7000 rpm
5-speed transmission
1760 lb, aluminum body w/tubular steel frame
coil-spring independent front suspension
transverse leaf-spring de Dion rear suspension

The 500 Testa Rossa was the last four-cylinder Ferrari sports car. This 500 TR was a one-off special for a princess.

Mondials scored some notable successes. One was Ascari and Luigi Villoresi placing second overall and first in class in the 12 Hours of Casablanca in December, 1953. The Mondial scored two more first-in-class wins in other North African races, one by the famed French driver, Maurice Trintignant, who finished second overall at Dakar.

In another fine showing, Vittorio Marzotto piloted a Mondial to second overall in the 1954 Mille Miglia and won the International Sports 2-liter class. Perhaps the Mondial's most magnificent victory was in the hands of Mike Hawthorn and Umberto Maglioli, who beat the 3-liter cars in a Grand Prix race at Monza.

The racing career of the 500 Mondial was short, just three years. And in some ways, it is another example of the Ferrari Barchetta. It was small, built on an 88.6-in. wheelbase, and lightweight. But time brought change. A new four-cylinder engine was introduced in 1956 in the 500 Testa Rossa, the last of the competition four-cylinder Ferraris.

JAGUAR D-TYPE

D-type Jaguars were the cars that stopped Ferrari wins in America. Sherwood Johnston won the 1955 C-Modified national championships, and Walt Hansgen took the next four titles in Briggs Cunningham prepared D-types.

The decade of the '50s was the great age of British racing. Jaguar emerged as the premier marque with the debut of the C-type in 1951. The C-type LeMans win of that year, in the face of nine Ferraris and 19 entries with larger engines, Cunningham and Allard, for instance, was a remarkable showing because only three C-Jags were entered.

The ever-present Aston Martin threat, five DB2s, provided intense rivalries among British entries in 1951 and, although not a threat, a single 1100cc Porsche was entered. This privately entered coupe marked the return of Germany to postwar racing.

LeMans '52 was the first postwar win by a German car, Mercedes

with a 1-2, and was a Jaguar fiasco that was not to be repeated the next year. The 3.4-liter C-types came back with a 1-2 finish in '53, although Ferrari posted the fastest lap for the second year straight.

With competition steadily increasing, Jaguar introduced the D-type in 1954. The drive train of the D-type was very similar to the final C-type, but a redesigned body produced a dramatic and more aerodynamic shape. It was possibly the most dynamic and charismatic of the classic Jaguars.

The D-types were built for the sole purpose of continuing Jaguar's wins, and later became production cars. Still later, they became the basis of the unfortunate XKSS that went up in smoke when the factory burned.

All the production D-Jags had short-nosed bodywork compared to

BONNEVILLE D-TYPE #529

This model D-type was delivered to a Lexington, Massachusetts dealer by Max Hoffman, the eastern United States Jaguar distributor. John Gordon Benett, a Cunningham team driver in D-types suggested that rising driving ace, Walter Hansgen, be selected to drive the car in amateur competition. Hansgen raced the car on a regional and national level in the northeast during the entire 1956 season, at Watkins Glen, Thompson, Cumberland, Lime Rock and other competitive tracks of the time.

He was highly successful, and that led to a seat on the Briggs Cunningham team. The car was parked when Hansgen left, and some years later a new owner, Tom Rutherford, acquired #529 and drove it to high school—among other things!

After a year of driving the car, Rutherford concluded that the car had world-record potential in the C/Sports Racing class and set about preparing the car for the Bonneville Salt Flats in Utah. His quest was a new land-speed record in his class.

Rutherford corresponded with "Lofty" England, then racing director for Jaguar, who responded with suggestions for preparing the car for speed-record attempts. With modifications made to the engine, wheels,

tires and covers and the car's bodywork, Rutherford's team arrived at Bonneville in August, 1960.

His team consisted of his mother, girlfriend and a buddy accompanied by a limited supply of tools and parts. Rutherford was just 19 years old, and this was his first world speed-record attempt. During the week, the team refined the car into shape to produce a two-way timed speed of 185.5 mph. Unfortunately, that was not quite enough for a new record, the C/Sports Racing record stood at 191 mph at the time.

However, Rutherford's timed speed has not been officially beaten in the succeeding years by other Jaguars. Thus, #529 remains officially as the fastest D-type, and to this day is the fastest timed Jaguar in two-way speed trials, although subsequent V12 road-racing Jaguars have no doubt exceeded that speed.

The present owner has restored #529 to its Bonneville specifications which consists of almost everything run by the Rutherford team. Lettering on the side corresponds to the way it ran back then, and the "Moon" wheel covers and Firestone high-speed slicks are original Rutherford equipment still in good condition today.

the longer Works cars. The aerodynamics and characteristic rear fin were largely the result of Malcolm Sayer, who joined Jaguar from the Bristol Aircraft Company. The chassis of the D-type retained tubular structures similar to the C-type, but with a strong monocoque center section that

proved itself at LeMans 1954. D-types were 20-mph faster that the C-types, and hit top speeds of 170 mph.

The famed Jaguar in-line six-cylinder engine was continued in the new cars and produced 250 HP from 3442cc, an increase of about 50 HP

Built upon the huge successes of the C-type Jaguars, D-types continued the British domination of LeMans through 1957. The rear fin was a characteristic of D-types that ran the famed Sarthe circuit for three victories, 1955, '56 and '57. The 1957 win set both speed and distance records that were not bettered until 1961. D-types were the last British victors at LeMans until 1975 when the Jackie Ickx/Derek Bell Gulf-Mirage DFV won. Here, Bib Stillwell takes some fast laps at a recent vintage-car race.

Jaguar twin-cam six is the heart of the British glory years of racing. Bore and stroke is 83 X 106mm for a displacement of 3442cc. Using a single sparkplug per cylinder and 9:1 compression, these engines produced 250 HP at 5750 rpm with Webers and 306 HP with fuel injection. Power was transferred via a triple-plate clutch and a four-speed transmission. A typical standing-start quarter-mile time was 13.7 seconds. Top speed was about 175 mph.

over the C-type.

In their debut at LeMans 1954, the 3.4-liter D-types battled it out magnificently with 4.9-liter Ferraris. After 24 hours of racing, Tony Rolt and Duncan Hamilton finished second, just one minute behind and one-tenth mph under the average speed of the winning Ferrari.

JAGUAR D-TYPE
1955

3442cc/210-CID DOHC in-line 6-cylinder
250 HP @ 5750 rpm
4-speed transmission
2020 lb, aluminum body, monocoque chassis w/tubular subframe, coil-spring independent front suspension, torsion-bar rear suspension

Placed into production in 1955, D-Types won many races and established their remarkable versatility in sports-car racing worldwide. As development continued, a variety of small running changes were incorporated. Most had no fin, whose primary function was high-speed stability at LeMans, but most D-Types retained their characteristic sloping rear cowling behind the driver, some with a faired-in head rest.

Future World Driver Champion, Mike Hawthorn, joined Jaguar as a Works driver in 1955. He replaced Moss, who was lured over to race the Mercedes 300SLRs with the great Juan Manuel Fangio. Independent teams, Briggs Cunningham in America and Ecurie Ecosse in Scotland, were to prove highly successful with the Jags. The Scottish team won both the 1956 and '57 LeMans 24-Hours in D-types driven by lead driver, Ron Flockhart, and set a distance record in 1957 that wasn't broken until 1961.

Cunningham's own cars had been Jaguar challengers prior to his association with the factory. His team of drivers, Phil Walters and Mike Hawthorn, took their Cunningham sponsored D-Type to victory in the 1955 Sebring 12-Hour. The Jaguar posted a new speed record, 79.4 mph vs. the previous year's 73.6 mph, and bested the Phil Hill/Carroll Shelby Ferrari 750 Monza.

The 1953 LeMans win by a C-type broke both the 100-mph and 2500-mile distance barriers for the first time. It was also a triumph for disc brakes. The trend was set and no LeMans enduro since has fallen under those figures. The 1955 LeMans first- and third-place D-type finish with an Aston Martin DB3S in second was marred by tragedy, but still recorded new records in both categories. The 1956 D-type win at LeMans was off the pace a bit, but the Flockhart/Ivor Bueb team paced the 1-2-3 D-Jag finish of 1957 with a resounding 113.85-mph average over 2732.23 miles, both new records.

Aircraft-inspired enclosed cockpit of the D-type is surrounded with a small windscreen. Right-hand drive, big dials behind a wood-rimmed steering wheel and left-hand shifter were the tools of champions.

Other D-type wins, both Works and non-Works cars, at Reims in 1954 and '56, Spa-Francorchamps, Montlhery, Goodwood and Silverstone established the Jags firmly in European racing. In America, Walt

Hansgen, a New York Jaguar dealer, won SCCA's C-Modified championship in a D-type in 1956 and '57, and the cars produced wins as late as 1960. Such was the durability of these magnificent cars. However, Sir William Lyons was most interested in LeMans and British events, so his Works Jaguars were not seen in other major European events. As a result, Mercedes-Benz won the World Sports Car Championship in 1955, followed by Ferrari in 1956 and '57 when the D-Jaguars were at their peak.

Although the D-type grew out of the earlier C-types, the cars were different in many ways. The earlier cars were built on a space frame while the D-Jags had monocoque construction of 18-gage magnesium. The front suspension was hung out on a tubular aluminum subframe like the C-type. The production-based, solid rear-axle assembly was positioned by four steel trailing arms bolted to the rear of the monocoque tub. Steering was rack and pinion. The disc brakes used three pairs of pads at the front and two pairs each at the rear.

The engine, a ten-year-old classic by 1957, used a cast-iron block with an aluminum-alloy, twin-cam head and a dry-sump oiling system. To further lower engine height, it was laid over at 8°. Carbureted versions of the 3.8-liter six were rated as high as 270 HP, but in fuel-injected form as raced by Cunningham, power rose to 306 HP.

Some people say a machine can never be art, but there is something very appealing about the Jaguar twin-cam six. The entire car is charismatic with its sweeping lines, that purposeful fin and clean bullet-like nose. They sold for $9875 when new and have gained in value ever since.

Bib Stillwell in Australia, John Gordon Bennet in the United States, Duncan Hamilton in Britain, to name only three, show the international appeal of the D-types. But it was Ron Flockhart driving for Ecurie Ecosse who gave D-types their greatest moments with two straight wins at LeMans.

MERCEDES-BENZ 300SLR

With its air brake up, the SLR was more than competitive with disc-brake, D-type Jaguars. The SLRs were extremely rugged racing cars. Photo courtesy of Mercedes-Benz.

The return of Mercedes to sports-car racing in 1952 brought a new dimension to international racing. With old-but-proven drivers, Caracciola (51), Lang (43) and Kling (40), the team took a 1-2-3 in the Swiss GP that was run as a sports-car race. Two finished LeMans 1-2. Following that, Lang won the German Grand Prix. The Mercedes-Benz team then finished 1-2 in Mexico's 1945-mile Carrera Panamericana enduro, serving notice that Germany was back.

Everyone was well aware of the prewar silver cars, and the new cars showed themselves to be every bit as capable. Although these were sports cars, M-B shifted emphasis to a full-scale Grand Prix effort when the board of directors authorized a GP program in 1954. Recalling the 300SL victory, Daimler-Benz's public-relations people dubbed the newcomer the 300SLR, but the car was more like M-B's enclosed W196 Grand

Prix car of that period rather than the earlier 300SL sports cars. The 300SLs were race-proven cars that led to production sports cars of that designation first appearing in 1954. Thoroughly engineered, these 145-mph production two-seaters were remarkable sports cars.

It was reported that Rudi Caracciola hit nearly 240 mph at the high-speed Avus track in a streamlined, eight-cylinder W125 Grand Prix car in 1937. In 1938, he averaged 268.9 mph in another car, a streamlined, 12-cylinder 5.6-liter car for an international kilometer class record, and posted 271.5 mph one way. That record still stands as the highest speed yet attained on a public road, the Frankfurt-Darmstadt autobahn.

Drawing on such experience and the new sports cars, the new Mercedes-Benz W196s raced in both open-wheel form for tight tracks and with enclosed bodies for long, fast Grand Prix courses. But, unlike their supercharged, 5.7-liter, 646-HP W125 prewar forebears, the W196 had a 2.5-liter, 280-HP engine of similar straight-8 design.

The highly tuned cars were temperamental and required precise

Juan Fangio and Stirling Moss, the two greatest drivers of modern times, raced these 300SLRs to resounding success and dominated sports-car racing. Road & Track photo by John Lamm.

The imposing rear view of the 300SLR was most often the Mercedes-Benz image competitors saw. Moss with Denis Jenkinson as navigator teamed for a spectacular win in the Mille Miglia of 1955. Their average pace of 98.5 mph was never broken in that Italian enduro. Road & Track photo by John Lamm.

The famed Mercedes-Benz 300SLR dominated sports-car racing in 1955 to win the World Sports Car Championship. It was brilliantly conceived and remains an enduring technical masterpiece. Juan Manuel Fangio won two of his five world driving titles in 1954 and '55 with the 2.5-liter Mercedes-Benz W196 GP car, the basis of the 3-liter 300SLR. Here, a 300SLR piloted by Phil Hill mixes it up with a D-Jag and Ferrari at a vintage-car race. Road & Track photo by John Lamm.

preparation, special oil, special fuel and sparkplug changes from start-up to racing. Even though they required special attention, the highly crafted, sophisticated cars proved to be overwhelming. The W196s won 12 of 15 races entered in 1954 and '55, took a 1-2 finish in seven races, won another with a 1-2-3, and yet another with a 1-2-3-4 sweep. The great Fangio took the World Driver's Championship both years in the cars, and Daimler-Benz AG won the Grand Prix, World Sports Car, American Sports Car and European Touring Car Championships in 1955.

Typical of Mercedes's advanced design, they were first to race at LeMans with fuel injection, but surprisingly did not equip SLRs with disc brakes. With huge inboard drums, the LeMans cars were assisted by an air brake—hydraulically operated lift-up rear body section. The air brake proved to be a rather controversial innovation, and was not used at many race tracks.

Known internally as the W196S, the SLR had 500cc more displacement than the GP cars. Its Hirth roller-bearing crank was similar, but the SLR's engine had cast rather than welded-up steel blocks like the W196 GP cars. The W196S block displaced 2982cc and was dead *square* with a 78 X 78mm bore and stroke. The block was actually two fours with a power takeoff in the middle to reduce crank flex. The flywheel was eliminated.

The DOHC straight-8 was laid over 33° to the horizontal for reduced front-end height. The engine featured *desmodromic* valve gear; both valve opening and closure were positive actuation and eliminated valve springs. The engine weighed a healthy 517 pounds complete, and produced as much as 302 HP. Factory engineers limited race revs to 7600 rpm, but reckoned the engine could go 2200 miles at 7800 rpm.

MERCEDES-BENZ 300SLR
1955

2982cc/182-CID DOHC in-line 8-cylinder w/desmodromic valves
302 HP @ 7800 rpm
5-speed transmission
1960 lb, aluminum body w/tubular frame
torsion-bar independent suspension front and rear

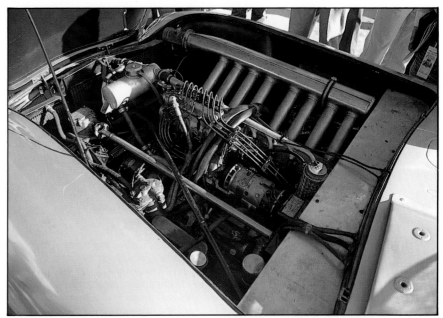

The SLR's fuel-injected, DOHC straight-eight W196S engine produced 275 HP from 2982cc. Of technical interest is the engine's Hirth roller-bearing crank and desmodromic valve gear. Road & Track photo by William Motta.

The cars were fitted with a five-speed transmission behind the differential. Engineers worked out gearing for each track and, typical of their attention to detail, they came within 1% of projected top speeds and lap times, allowing 0.3 seconds per shift. In the 24 Hours of LeMans, the SLR could touch 175 mph. But the big cars yielded considerably to the acceleration of the 3.4-liter, six-cylinder D-Jags and 4.4-liter, six-cylinder Ferrari 121 LM that paced the race with a speed of 181.25 mph.

At LeMans, five D-Jaguars were entered, three of them were long-nose Works cars, and were led by the Hawthorn/Bueb and Rolt/Hamilton teams. In the Ferrari stable were five entries. One was driven by a young American driver, Phil Hill, who received his first LeMans experience in the powerful big-six Ferrari. But, like the D-Jags, Ferrari factory team and a Cunningham private entry, Hill did not finish.

The Fangio/Moss team were the leading drivers along with the Fitch/Levegh and Kling/Simon teams in two other Mercedes SLRs. As shown in the early running, LeMans 1955 would have been another great day for Mercedes-Benz were it not for the disaster that remains motor racing's worst accident.

1955, YEAR OF DISASTER

Throughout the history of racing, only a few cars have emerged as singular achievements of technical brilliance. The Mercedes-Benz 300SLR is one. It's unfortunate, however, that the glory of such a great car is marred by tragedy.

The overwhelming successes of the cars is a matter of record, yet part of their history will forever include the 81 lives lost at LeMans in 1955. In addition to the LeMans disaster is the role played by another Mercedes, a 300SL, in the disaster at Dundrod in Britain's Tourist Trophy also in that year.

LEMANS DISASTER

The entry list promised an exciting race. Three SLRs were entered with a truly international team of drivers. The lead twosome, Fangio/Moss, were Argentine and British. Pierre Levegh and John Fitch were a French/American team, and another Frenchman, Andre Simon, drove with the German, Karl Kling. Levegh's real name was actually Bouillon. He had proven himself well in the 1952 Mercedes-Benz triumph at LeMans by driving a Talbot solo and leading for some 23 of the 24 hours.

Five D-Jags and five Ferraris, a Briggs Cunningham team Jaguar along with an Offenhauser-powered C-6R of his own marque, faced the three SLRs at the start. Aston Martin was present with their threatening DB3S cars along with two Works Maseratis. MG made its return to racing, their first showing since 1935, and ran three EX-182 prototypes based on the soon-to-be-introduced MGA. Another important newcomer was a Lotus IX driven by Ron Flockhart and Colin Chapman.

Of the 60 starting entrants, 27 were British. At the end, there were 21 finishers. Hawthorn set the fastest lap, 122.39 mph, and he and Ivor Bueb won, setting both a new distance record (2569.60 miles) and a new average speed record (107.07 mph).

Some 200,000 spectators were packed-in tightly along the circuit. Just after the first pit stops, disaster struck. Hawthorn had just passed Lance Macklin's Austin-Healey when he chose to pit and cut across Macklin's line. Macklin swerved left into the path of Levegh who was preparing to pass at high speed. That set up the disaster. Levegh hit the Austin-Healey's tail and was deflected into a safety barrier across the track. He was killed in the violent impact and subsequent explosion. The engine, front suspension and other parts were launched into the crowd. It took a while for the full horrors to be realized. The final death toll came to 81, and more than 20 injured.

This was the single worst accident in the history of racing and had extensive repercussions on both LeMans and racing itself. Motor racing was banned temporarily in France while a lengthy inquiry into the cause of the accident was conducted. The outcome was that no single factor could be blamed, but drastic changes for both the race and the circuit were required.

TOURIST TROPHY DISASTER

The Tourist Trophy was one of the oldest races held, tracing its origin to 1905. It was first run over the tortuous roads of the Isle of Man. Between the world wars, the circuit was moved to Ards in Ulster, as noted earlier. After a Riley crashed into the crowd, the TT was moved to Donington Park. For 1950, the race returned to Ulster, but this time it was run over the twisty, narrow roads of Dundrod. It was called "7.3 miles of hell," and was the scene of a succession of accidents in 1955 that saw the end of the TT there.

The year 1955 was the Golden Jubilee edition of the TT and was run without handicap; the fastest finisher won. Like LeMans, a prestigious Index award was formulated that gave any entrant a shot at a noteworthy prize. It attracted many top teams.

The TT was the next to last event on the World Sports Car Championship calendar. Following the withdrawal of the SLR team at LeMans, and a subsequent win by Jaguar, Mercedes-Benz entered three SLRs in an attempt to gain valuable points toward the Championship.

Fangio, Moss, Kling, Fitch, von Trips and Simon were the drivers for Mercedes against the Jaguars, Astons, Ferraris, Maseratis and other cars. Newcomers Cooper and Lotus went head-to-head along with Porsches that had shown themselves to be strong long-distance performers by finishing fourth (a 550 Spyder) at LeMans.

On the second lap, the slower moving 300SL coupe of Vicomte de Barry straddled the middle of the road and backed up faster cars. Other drivers had to take chances when passing. Ivor Bueb squeezed by in his works Cooper by putting two wheels on the grass, but when Jim Mayers tried the same in his Cooper, he lost control and crashed into a concrete gate pillar. Bursting into flames, the wreckage fell back onto the track in the path of Ken Wharton's Fraser-Nash. Wharton crashed and was thrown from his car, which also burst into flames. The next car, driven by Bill Smith, also hit the roadside bank, throwing its driver out. Then, a Porsche crashed, followed by Lance Macklin's Austin-Healey.

Macklin's involvement in a second tragic accident caused him to walk away from the carnage with helmet in hand never to race seriously again. Jim Mayers, whose co-driver was Jack Brabham, was not as fortunate. Scotsman Bill Smith, only 20, was also not as fortunate. He had displayed driving brilliance described to be that shown later by Jimmy Clark, but his luck ran out.

Later in the race, Richard Mainwaring lost control of his works Elva and crashed in flames for the third tragic misfortune of the Tourist Trophy.

LeMans was the most significant road race in the world, and some claimed the TT to be a close second. In both cases, 1955 was a sad year overshadowed by disaster. Mercedes-Benz won the World Sports Car Championship that year, and even though a team of cars was planned for the 1956 season, the fabulous SLR retired.

Chevrolet management were promoting.

With a growing following, Corvette sales rose from 674 in 1955 to 3467 in '56 and 6339 in '57 to 9168 in '58. But the cars also grew progressively heavier, to 3085 pounds in 1958.

Throughout the late 1950s and early '60s, Corvettes were the mainstay of American sports-car racing. By then, Chevrolet Division had built a solid base of performance parts. Although not officially racing, Ed Cole had promoted Chevrolet performance and encouraged corporate ties with successful teams.

CORVETTE
1957

4639cc/283-CID fuel-injected OHV V8
283 HP @ 6000 rpm
4-speed transmission, 2890 lb, fiberglass body w/box steel frame
coil-spring independent front suspension
leaf-spring, live-axle rear suspension

Not only was that good for enthusiasts who wanted to "race American," it was good business for Chevrolet. A lot of competition testing went into engineering development of performance parts. From the engineering side, vehicle dynamics under heavy braking and hard cornering gave important information used to improve handling of production cars. With the rigors imposed on parts during racing, a great deal is learned very quickly about their strength and durability. One race would very likely point out a faulty part that might not show up under normal conditions for years. Thus, Corvette racers have contributed to better parts from Chevrolet and Chevrolet has continually provided a wide variety of heavy-duty parts for all sorts of racing.

That provided a long and illustrious career for Corvette racing on American tracks. However, the cars did not emerge as world-class sports/racing cars with overwhelming wins on European circuits. Their best showing at LeMans, for instance, was the Briggs Cunningham team of three Corvettes entered in the 5-liter GT class of 1960. The Bob Grossman/John Fitch car finished eighth overall, winning the class by posting a race average of 97.92 mph for 2350.03 miles.

However, that was the only Corvette top-10 placing at LeMans during the 1956 to 1965 era and represents the sparse racing achievements by the marque in international racing.

But, SCCA racing in America was another story. Corvettes were almost unbeatable until the unleashing of Carroll Shelby's Cobras in 1963, and later the Shelby GT-350 Mustang and Sunbeam Tiger. Not only were they popular racing cars, Vettes became immensely popular street cars and are universally recognized as the great American dream machine. The Corvette is the best known American car ever built.

Such response is testimony to the huge success that is Corvette. Throughout its history, it has had a continual following. It is no doubt the all-time most popular sports car, a lasting legacy that spans many other marques that have come and gone and slipped into obscurity.

After Ford's Thunderbird went to a four-seat design in 1958, Corvette was left alone as America's only production sports car. High styling, comfort and sizzling performance in a striking two-place roadster of immense appeal was what made Corvette the great American dream machine.

For 1957, single and dual 4-bbl 283-CID engines were offered in Corvettes. The two 4-bbl engine with 270 HP at 6000 rpm provided unmatched street performance, except from the sensational 283-HP fuel-injected version available that year. With the fuelie, 0—60 mph came up in 7.2 seconds with a top speed of over 130 mph.

AC ACE

The AC Ace was one of Britain's top performing 2-liter roadsters of the late 1950s. AC dealer Ken Rudd installed a 2-liter Bristol engine derived from the prewar BMW 328 and produced the first AC-Bristol. Later factory models for the road received that engine, and the factory built perhaps 24 specially equipped cars for racing. One is shown here with yellow racing markings.

Introduction of the Ace line of lightweight sports cars was in 1953. About a year later, the Aceca Coupe was added to round out AC's sports machines. It seemed that overnight, the staid company of AC Cars Ltd. transformed itself with exciting sports cars. The new cars earned many victories over their production lifetime, beginning with the first production Ace taking a class win in the Tulip Rally. That Ace went on to a great career in the hands of Bob "sideways" Staples and Ken Rudd, and provided AC Cars with a lot of exposure for its products.

Later, the need for more power to remain competitive brought about the use of two other engines. One was the more-powerful Bristol unit, and finally the use of the even stronger Ford Zephyr six.

Bodywork of the new Ace was lightweight aluminum fitted over a tubular-steel subframe, Superleggera style. And, like the Jaguar XK-120, the Ace was an immediate success—a handsome roadster begging to be driven very fast. It was priced between the Jaguar and Austin-Healey Hundred.

In British measure, the Ace in GT trim weighed 16.5 hundredweight. In America, that is 1848 pounds (hundredweight equals 112 pounds). Extended road testing showed the car capable of better than 25 miles per gallon and a top speed exceeding 100 mph.

The factory offered extensive racing options for enthusiasts to upgrade performance. With both a roadster and a coupe, AC Cars was well on its way to a sports-racing tradition. In perhaps the Ace's best showing with the AC six-cylinder engine, Dressel and Woodbury finished 18th overall, completing 154 laps in the Sebring 12-Hours in

In final form, the Bristol 100D2 six-cylinder produced 130 HP at 5750 rpm. Fitted with triple Solex carburetors, the cast-iron block and alloy-head engine was rather high but the profile of the Ace body concealed it nicely. For these rare factory-prepared race cars, the engine was designated the 100D2C and delivered about 136 HP and over 130 mph.

1956 for an average of 66.7 mph.

However, racing showed the cars to be underpowered. A variety of engine modifications increased output, but it was clear that the Ace and Aceca coupe needed a new engine to remain competitive.

One of the spoils of World War II was a new engine that found a home in these cars. After the fall of Nazi Germany, Sir Roy Feddon, technical advisor to the British government on aircraft matters, studied the prewar BMW 328 engine with increasing interest. As war reparations, the designs were transferred to the Bristol Aircraft Company and to Frazer-Nash.

Fritz Fiedler had designed BMW's 1971cc in-line six-cylinder engine, a powerful and rugged design. Producing 120 HP at 5500 rpm from a compression ratio of 9.6:1 in racing tune, Feddon recognized that Fiedler's engine had potential, and redesigned derivatives of the BMW 2-liter duly appeared from Bristol.

With a single internal cam operating inclined valves through a complicated but effective pushrod and rocker assembly, the tall and narrow Bristol engine developed 85 HP in basic form. With some racing preparation, it could achieve 150 HP. Its aluminum head was fitted to a four-main-bearing, cast-iron block with a Nitrided crankshaft.

Ken Rudd was the first to fit a Bristol engine into an Ace. He proceeded to trounce the cars that had been troublesome when he was running the lower-powered AC engine. After winning the British Production Sports Car Championship in 1956 with the car, AC Cars lost no time in making the Bristol engine available to its customers. The engine

was expensive and the price of the AC-Bristol exceeded the price of the XK-120 Jaguar as first offered. The factory cautioned buyers that the Bristol option was really meant for racing.

Running the 100D2 Bristol six, Robert Kuhn won SCCA's E-Production class in 1957 in an Ace. In this form, the engine developed 125 HP at 5750 rpm and gave a top speed of over 115 mph.

In the AC-Bristol's first showing at Sebring in 1957, the Fernandez and Droulers team completed 161 laps, finishing 17th overall while winning the under 2-liter class, with an average speed of 69.77 mph. In the 1958 race, Stear, Norris and Harris ran 168 laps in the 12 hours to average 72.8 mph to finish 15th overall and three more AC-Bristols finished 16th, 19th and 22nd. The 1959 race saw the AC-Bristol move up a notch finishing 14th overall but at a lower pace while 2 other AC-Bristols finished 22nd and 24th.

Ken Rudd thought the car to have a good chance at LeMans, and

AC BRISTOL
1958

1971cc/120-CID OHV in-line 6-cylinder
130 HP @ 5750 rpm
4-speed transmission, 1685 lb, aluminum body w/tubular frame
transverse leaf-spring independent suspension front and rear

prepared a roadster that he and Peter Bolton drove to 10th overall and second in class in 1957. They completed 2350 miles and averaged 97 mph with fuel consumption around 16 mpg. Top speed was shown to be 130 mph.

Thus encouraged, AC Cars decided to make a works car for Le-Mans 1958 and built a 1395-pound Bristol-powered special. Topping out at 154 mph along the Mulsanne, the sleek AC finished eighth overall, ahead of a private-entry AC-Bristol in ninth overall. In the 1959 race, run in tremendous heat that sidelined many other cars, Whiteway and Turner were the only finishers in class and took a seventh overall at an average of 95.38 mph for 2289.65 miles.

To add to the AC-Bristol's long list of laurels, it captured SCCA's E-Production class championship amid grumblings from competitors that caused SCCA to consider reclassifying the car into D-Production. When an AC-Bristol won the E-Production championship in 1959, SCCA did reclassify the car. But to no avail. The cars won the championship against Healey Hundreds and Mercedes-Benz 300 SLs that year, and with a further bump into C-Production, the AC-Bristol faced Jaguar XK-120s and Corvettes. Against such cars of considerably more power, the AC-Bristol came back to win the C-P championship in 1960!

In 1958, the factory built some two dozen AC-Bristol competition cars that weighed under 1400 pounds. These cars were powered by 2-liter Bristol 100D2C engines in the highest state of tune, about 135 HP, and achieved a top speed of 132 mph. Their bodies were ultra-lightweight aluminum alloy weighing about 60 pounds.

LOTUS, FLOWERING OF GENIUS

Elite's suspension was derived from Formula 2 cars. The aerodynamic Lotus Elite excelled in GT class racing as shown by one winning its class in the 1960 Tourist Trophy and another that won the *Autosport* championship among a long succession of other wins.

The Lotus Elite was a smashing success when first shown at the Earls Court motor show in 1957. The fiberglass Grand Touring coupe was heralded the star of the show.

Another example of the coming of purpose-built racing cars during the mid-1950s was the cars from Colin Chapman. Lotus Cars Ltd. was founded in 1955 by Chapman, who designed, built and raced his early creations. Although designers, builders and drivers are usually separate lots, Chapman proved his abilities in each area and harried many a top-ranking driver with equal skill at times.

In the late 1950s, Chapman retired from driving to concentrate on building his cars and to manage his growing Team Lotus. That proved to be another of his considerable talents as Team Lotus brought home seven World Manufacturer's Championships. Only Ferrari equals that number.

In 1958, Chapman entered Formula 1 racing. The car in this first effort was not designed for that class, but since then, about one-fourth of all races entered have been won by Lotus cars. Chapman's revolutionizing influence has also been felt at Indianapolis with the mid-engine

PORSCHE SPYDERS

From humble beginnings, the Porsche progressively advanced into more competitive racing toward eventual overall wins at LeMans and world championships with later cars.

The huge success that became the racing Spyders took shape in the form of Dr. Ernst Fuhrmann's brilliantly conceived four-cam, four-cylinder, air-cooled engine.

The engine Dr. Fuhrmann designed, known as the Type 547, was a technical masterpiece. Designed in 1952, the engine was his answer to the increasing competition from OSCA and other 1.1- and 1.5-liter cars. Dr. Fuhrmann's four-cammer had so much designed-in performance potential that it became Porsche's mainline racing engine through 1965. In final form, the boxer-4 powered Porsche's highly successful Type 904 sports/racing coupe a full decade after its inception.

In first form, the Type 547 engine produced 110 HP at 7800 rpm. Its block and heads were cast aluminum. The crank was a Hirth roller and the DOHC cams on each bank were shaft-driven. The 547 was a twin-ignition, twin-plug design that was a nightmare to assemble. But once completed, it repeatedly proved to be a rugged engine capable of taking on anything in its class. And it usually won.

Further development of the engine took it to over 180 HP in later Porsche F-1 and F-2 cars. Using tube-frame construction of the 550 Spyders, the four-cammers powered factory-built racing cars throughout the racing world.

The 550s were Porsche's first real racers. They were offered to the public at around $7000; a good value for the racing dollar at the time. The virtue of the 550, its balance, proved to be the undoing of many competitors who found the cars more nimble than bigger-bore cars and more durable than lighter ones.

Among their first entries into racing were a team of two 550s at LeMans 1953. They ran older pushrod engines and were fitted with makeshift aluminum tops for better aerodynamics. Although not powered by Type 547 four-cam engines, the cars served notice that Porsche was a contender in small-engine classes. The two were clocked at better than 122 mph, and one posted a 1.5-liter class victory by completing the 24 hours at an average speed of 86.3 mph.

The Porsche 550 Spyder was the factory's first entry into purpose-built racing cars. Introducing Dr. Ernst Fuhrmann's superb four-cam air-cooled four-cylinder in 1954, the 550s soon became the scourge of production sports-car racing in the 1.5-liter class and frequently outperformed more-powerful cars.

Compact Type 547 Fuhrmann four-cam displaced 1498cc from a bore and stroke of 85 X 66mm. With a compression ratio of 9.5:1, first works engines of 1954 produced 112 HP at 7000 rpm. Advanced features included crossflow hemispherical combustion chambers, dry-sump lubrication, twin ignition, a roller crankshaft, aluminum-alloy crankcase and heads, and shaft-driven cams. The engine ended its factory racing lifetime on a high note in the Type 904 coupe of 1964.

Two-place 550 sports roadster combined exhilarating performance and superb racing potential as shown by a 1.5-liter class win at LeMans 1955. It also won the Biennial Cup and the Index of Performance, averaging 99.15 mph for 2379.68 miles and finished fourth overall.

The first significant placing of a Porsche at LeMans had been in 1951 when a 356 placed 20th overall and won the 1100cc class. From that victory, Porsche steadily grew into a leading contender in international racing at high levels and took more LeMans victories than any other marque to date.

96

PORSCHE 550 SPYDER
1955

1498cc/91-CID DOHC air-cooled flat 4-cylinder
112 HP @ 7000 rpm
5-speed transmission, 1300 lb, aluminum body w/box steel frame
all-independent suspension

The 550 Spyders contributed to Porsche's increasing LeMans fortunes with a succession of wins as the Fuhrmann four-cammer proved itself by taking the 1.5-liter class from 1954 through 1958. Porsches with similar 1.6- and 2.0-liter engines took class victories from 1960 through '65 when the four-cammer was replaced by a new six-cylinder that launched Porsche toward overall victory at LeMans.

Not only did the four-cam engine power Porsche to LeMans class wins, it scored class victories in the Mille Miglia, at Nurburgring, the Tour de France, Sebring, the Targa Florio, Carrera Panamericana and in rallies and hill climbs. Wherever racing was done, Porsche's Type 547 engine in its many variations was usually well in front of its class and nipping at the heels of more-powerful cars.

These Porsches became so dominant that it took another Porsche to beat them. The 550 Spyders were racing cars sold in enough volume to be classified as production cars. Most were exported to the United States where they took SCCA class championships. Several drivers, the famed Ken Miles for instance, claimed the Spyders to be the best overall racing car of their time.

Because 550 Spyders were well received in America, other marques responded with their versions. British lightweights became a force that Porsche engineers had to reckon with. Stuttgart's response was the 550A of 1956. The four-cam engine with more power was fitted to an all-new chassis. The 550A Porsches also received a new five-speed transmission, although it was really a four-speed with a starting-line low for quick starts. The new cars were built on a proper tubular space-frame chassis rather than the previous ladder type. It was stronger, more rigid, and lighter. With attention to weight reduction everywhere, the 550A Spyders weighed in at around 1170 pounds. These new, more-powerful cars were in every way an improvement over earlier models. One major factor was an improved suspension that significantly reduced the problems of high-speed bump control inherent in the older design.

A later development of the 550 is this 550A/1500 RS, an even more potent Porsche, really an all-new car fitted with the proven Boxer-4 power train. With a proper tubular chassis and lighter weight, the 550A Spyder boasted 135 HP at 7200 rpm.

Still-later development of the Boxer-4 powered Porsche Spyder is this 1958 Type 718 RSK. Power was increased to 150 HP at 7800 rpm.

The 550As received Weber carbs and produced 135 HP at 7200 rpm on a compression ratio of 9.8:1. Bold challenges proved the new car to have a lot of potential, convincingly demonstrated by Umberto Maglioli who entered the grueling Targa Florio of '56. He single-handedly drove to overall victory, the second fastest finish up to that time and just 2.8 mph off the average set by Moss and Collins in their 3-liter Mercedes-Benz 300SLR the year before.

Porsche took a 1-2-3 class victory in the Reims 12-Hour over 2-liter Ferraris and continually showed the small, silver cars to be stiff competition. But just as the 550A was a response to increased efforts from other marques, another variation on the four-cam theme was introduced in 1957. That was the Type 718 RSK.

Although a rather complete redesign of the chassis, suspension and body rated only a letter designation when the 550 went to the 550A, the 718 got a complete redesignation when a tube was added to that same space frame. The body changed a little, but spectators were not likely to recognize the differences except for the advent of rear fins. Outwardly, the 718 was lower by about 5 inches and significantly sleeker.

Like all racing Porsches, the 718s received all sorts of improvements as the cars were really racing test beds for new ideas. All of the Spyders, the 550s, 718s and later RS60 and 61s, were built slightly differently in detail compared to other cars of their type because they were hand-built and incorporated ideas learned in the course of racing.

The 718 RSK carried the Porsche banner through 1959 when it was replaced by the RS60, a sophisticated and well-developed racer. The four-cam Spyder theme was well proven by then and both the RS60 and later RS61 were efforts at refining proven design rather than exploring new innovations.

With the Spyders, Porsche as a racing marque became established throughout the world. As a manufacturer originating in the late 1940s, much of the success of Porsche sales rested on racing acclaim and that rested on Dr. Fuhrmann's engine. Porsches became winners both on and off the track.

Two RSKs finished third and fourth overall at LeMans 1958, a remarkable finish with only 1.5 liters. One fact of note is that the third-place car ran a 1587cc four-cam engine and won the 2000cc class with stats of 101.22 mph for 2429.34 miles. Another four-cammer was fifth ahead of two Ferrari 250 TRs and a 2-liter AC Ace. With that showing, Porsche's reputation as the giant killer was well underway.

In 1963, a 718 finished eighth overall for the last significant LeMans showing of a Porsche Spyder. The following years, 1964 and '65, type 904 GTS coupes emerged as the dominant Porsche and were the factory's mainline racing car. The 718 of Linge and Barth averaged 104.86 mph for 2516.70 miles.

Such figures show that the Fuhrmann engine did indeed have huge reserve potential. Along with improved chassis as the Spyders evolved, an increased average pace of about 25 mph at LeMans was shown from the first four-cam 550 in 1954 to the 718 of 1963.

ASTON MARTIN DB3S

The Aston Martin DB3S was conceived in the winter of 1952—53 as David Brown (the DB designation) stepped up his racing stakes. Frank Feeley designed the body and the first prototype was tested at Monza in 1953.

Throughout the 1950s, David Brown's Aston Martins were very much a factor in sports-car racing. His was a commitment to win LeMans and many frustrating attempts were made. Frustrating because it took a decade to realize the goal.

David Brown, a trained engineer, controlled a complex of industries inherited from his family and traceable to his grandfather. Among them were the purchase of Aston Martin in 1947, then Lagonda in '48.

The purpose for the buyouts was twofold: a rescue attempt to keep such fine cars in manufacture and to have some fun. A Lagonda powered by a new engine designed by W.O. Bentley was in the offing when the Lagonda firm came upon hard times. Brown saw the mating of that engine in Astons to be an interesting combination. The Lagonda purchase went through at around $145,000 and the engine was installed in Astons, creating the DB2.

Brown had been a racing driver of some note early in life, winning hillclimbs and sand races in a supercharged Vauxhall Villiers, and now saw his Aston Martins competitive in sports-car racing. With a 2-liter, four-cylinder in a specially prepared DB1 Aston Martin, a rather surprising win in the Spa 24-Hour Sports Car race in 1948 launched Brown into a new racing tradition. When the 2.6-liter, DOHC six designed by Bentley was installed, Aston Martins were really in the thick of it.

The largest entry at LeMans 1949, by a single marque, was the six Astons entered, one being a new DB2. None won, but one did take seventh overall and third in class. Such finishes set the tone for many disappointing future races.

LeMans in 1950 saw no less than 25 French contenders along with three DB2 Astons and the first appearance of Jaguar with three XK120s. But this was the year of the Talbot-Lagos of Louis Rosier and son that set new records in average speed (89.71 mph) and distance (2153.12 miles).

However, adding encouragement to the Aston Martin effort was the fifth overall by George Abecassis and Lance Macklin whose bone-stock DB2 took the 3-liter class and shared the Index of Performance with a French Monopole-Panhard. This race showed that British racing was

In its first season, 1953, the DB3S took five impressive wins, but the following year was disappointing. 1955 produced a return to big wins with six major victories, but LeMans remained ever illusive.

Smooth lines and all-business cockpit of the DB3S show a large Smith's chronometric tach that operates in ticks of 100 rpm rather than smooth needle motion. At Rouen, 1956, Roy Salvadori drove this car to a fifth overall. It also took a fifth overall in the Empire Trophy of 1957 and finished 10th in the Nurburgring 1000 Km that year.

on the rise when 14 of 16 British entries finished with four taking class wins, led by the Allard/Cole third-place finish.

John Wyer had joined Aston Martin in 1950 as racing manager, and his cars would, in time, become top winners. With his DB2s looking good, the more-sophisticated DB3 was conceived for the 1952 season. Eighteen entries produced only one win, the Goodwood 9-Hour, and seven top-five finishes.

Then came the DB3S in 1953, a serious step toward overall wins. These cars were designed by Willie Watson with curvaceous coachwork by Frank Feeley. The DB3S wasn't ready for Sebring and Wyer's team barely lost to a Cunningham C-4R with a DB3. But shortly thereafter, the DB3S arrived on the scene and the Astons turned in five other wins, the British Empire Trophy, Silverstone, Charterhall, the Goodwood 9-Hour and the Dundrod TT, all races the DB3S entered after LeMans.

For 1954, a 4.5-liter V12 engine was produced for a Lagonda racing effort that earned no significant results. Neither did the DB3S in '54, except one win at Silverstone, a very disappointing season. Aston Martin was spread too thin that year for a well-developed racing team, but 1955 was a different story. DB3S Astons took first and second at Silverstone, first at Spa, finished second at LeMans, were 1-2-3-4 at Aintree, first at Crystal Palace, the Goodwood 9-Hour, and took Oulton Park.

By 1956, the DB3S had reached its peak, and another car—the DBR1—was underway. The DBR1 began a new era for David Brown, but not before the DB3S notched three more wins—Roy Salvadori at Silverstone, Moss at Oulton Park and Tony Brooks at Goodwood. The cars also scored seven seconds in impressive finishes.

The beautiful DB3S Aston Martins had the potential to win the big one, LeMans, but always seemed to come up short. They first raced the 24-Hours in 1953 with a poor showing, and after 12 factory entries through '56, their best was a second in both the 1955 and 1956 races. Even so, Brown and Wyer didn't give up.

In 1954, a strong Aston Martin entry of five cars plus the V12 Lagonda—really two doubled-up DB engines—showed Brown's interest was increasing. However, the Parnell/Salvadori supercharged DB3S (running a Wade blower delivering 10 pounds of boost and 240 HP) was the last to retire, having outlasted several formidable Ferraris.

They were back for the 1955 race, three DB3S Astons and the V12 Lagonda. Although marred by disaster, the race saw the Collins/Frere DB3S finish second overall, winning the 3-liter class. The following year the Moss and Collins DB3S finished second overall again and also won the 3-liter class just 10 miles behind the winning 3.4-liter D-Jag of Flockhart and Sanderson. For the '57 race, Colas and Kerguen finished 11th with another 3-liter class win in their DB3S.

That was the last year of successful DB3S Astons at LeMans. The all-conquering DBR1 followed the DB3S and became David Brown's first

In Nurburgring form, the DB3S 3-liter DOHC six-cylinder produced 231 HP at 6000 rpm from a compression ratio of 8.5:1. Bore and stroke of 84 X 90mm gave a displacement of 2992cc. Three 45 DCO Webers feed a twin-plug alloy head with valves inclined at 60°. The four-speed transmission is the Type 430/22.

ASTON MARTIN DB3S
1956

2992cc/183-CID DOHC in-line 6-cylinder
231 HP @ 6000 rpm
4-speed transmission
2061 lb, aluminum body w/large-tube ladder frame
trailing-link torsion bar front independent suspension
de Dion rear axle

DB3S/10 retains its original engine now producing about 240 HP, some 60 more than the 19 customer model DB3S cars with single-plug heads.

This engine was the W.O. Bentley design with valves inclined at 60°. It strongly influenced the design of the later DBR1 engine that placed Aston Martin in the forefront of world sports-car racing.

This particular DB3S uses a ladder frame with a deDion tube in the rear, Aston's latest development in chassis design at the time, and is the only one fitted with a wishbone front suspension found in later-production DB4 sports cars. Total weight is around 1800 pounds and performance shows 0—100 mph in around 14 seconds.

Although the works cars were DBR1s in 1958, they failed at Le-Mans and a DB3S was the second-place finisher in the hands of the Whitehead brothers who averaged 102.03 mph for 2448.75 miles behind the winning Gendebien/Hill Ferrari 250 TR. This DB3S is thought to be that car, the last of the works DB3S Astons.

In July, 1955, Wyer was named technical director at Aston Martin and his first challenge was to investigate a new DOHC six-cylinder engine to replace the DB3S. This was to be the engine that brought David Brown his goal of victory at LeMans. It had also become clear that an entirely new car was required and Wyer's team responded to the increasingly stronger challenges from Ferrari with the DBR1, David Brown's greatest sports-racing car.

LeMans winner and also won the World Sports Car Championship, the only British car to do so.

The car shown here is the last of 10 works DB3S Astons built, and shows Aston's beautiful jade green color. Fitted with the high-performance, dual-plug, aluminum-alloy head, power as raced in 1956 was 230 HP at 6000 rpm on a compression ratio of 8.5:1. Bore and stroke of 83x90mm produced 2922cc capacity.

JOHN WYER

"After the war, I was running a business that specialized in the preparation of racing and high-performance cars, Monaco Motors in Watford, England. Conditions were difficult, with gas rationing and all sorts of restrictions, and when my partners and I had the opportunity to sell the business at a profit we jumped at it. About that time, word came to me that David Brown at Aston Martin was looking for a team manager, and since I had some money from the sale of our business, I thought I could spend a year doing something I wanted to do before I settled down to a more serious career.

"At my first interview with David Brown, we agreed to a one-year contract which suited both of us. I went to Aston Martin as racing manager in 1950 and stayed for thirteen years. During that time, I progressed up the ladder to Technical Director and still later, General Manager.

"David Brown was rather like a benevolent dictator, and my job was to give him what he wanted which was to win races, particularly Le Mans and the Tourist Trophy. It was a very good association for me because David Brown gave me a great deal of freedom provided I delivered the goods.

"We introduced the DB3S in 1953 and won a lot of races with it through 1956. Like Jaguar, the engine was based on a production block, but Jaguar had the good sense to design theirs with somewhat more capacity which could be increased. Ours was limited to 3 liters and we were always at a disadvantage.

"We realized that a purpose-built racing engine was needed and in 1957 we brought out the DBR1 with the RB6 engine. That was a very good car which won the Nurburgring 1000 Km three times, the Tourist Trophy and, in 1959, the 24-Hours of LeMans, the one which really counted. In 1959 we also won the World Sports Car Championship, and then decided to withdraw from racing.

"Around the beginning of the 1960s, I was thinking that I was about as far as I could go with Aston Martin and began casting about for something more serious. Then the offer from Ford came along, and I joined them in 1963 for development of the GT-40. That was very different from working for David Brown because all decisions were made by committee and usually changed several times.

"After some early problems, Ford realized that beating Ferrari was not as easy as it sounded and began to treat it more seriously. They won LeMans twice, in 1966 and 1967, with the 7-liter engine. In 1967, they were a bit lucky because Ferrari was very close in second and third. After that, Ford was quite relieved to withdraw. I then took over the program with my own company, J. W. Automotive Engineering. I had always believed that the small-block engine, 4.7 or 5.0 liters, was the way to go, and we developed the original GT-40 into an exceptionally fine racing car. We won LeMans in 1968 and 1969 and the World Championship in 1968.

"At Sebring 1969, Porsche asked me to run their 917 program for 1970 and '71, so we rather stopped development of our Mirage cars which were to have been the GT-40 replacement. Porsche was a dramatic contrast to Ford. Everything was controlled by the Engineering Department, but they gave us a surprising amount of latitude to make changes. One of them was our change of the rear section of the 917 into a configuration which became known at Porsche as the "John Wyer" tail. The cars were then extremely stable at high speeds. In this form, the 917K won LeMans in 1970 and 1971, and our Gulf-Porsche 917s won the World Championship in both years.

"After that, I semi-retired in 1972 and left the day-to-day operation to John Horsman, but we continued development of the DFV Cosworth Mirage and won LeMans in 1975, along with third place, and the same two cars finished second and fifth in 1976.

"I've been very lucky because, most of my life I have been able to do the things which interested me most and being paid to do them was a bonus."

1969
Ferodo Gold Trophy for the most outstanding British performance of the year, a prestigious award granted to other automotive people of note, Keith Duckworth, Mike Hewland and Tony Vandervell (Vanwall), for instance.

1969
Gold Metal of the British Automobile Racing Club.

Honorary Member: British Racing Drivers Club and of the Club International des Anciens Pilotes de Grand Prix.

Chartered Engineer and a Fellow of the Institution of Mechanical Engineers.

MASERATI 2-LITER

The Tipo 52 Maserati came in two forms, the 200S and the 200SI. Both were open DOHC 4-cylinder cars with the SI being intended for international competition, thus the I designation. Wheelbase of the 200S was shortened by 50 mm for the SI, giving a 22-lb weight reduction.

In the last half of the 1950s, true road racing over normal roads was fast dying out. The attendant hazards—curbs and trees and no real protective barriers along spectator-lined trek, and unexpected occurrences such as a herd of goats or a farm hay wagon around the next bend—were recognized as posing unacceptable risks; thus the end of road racing.

Italy was the last bastion of real road racing where towns would sponsor events, probably to bring in tourists and world-class excitement. Bari, on the Adriatic coast, was among the last to hold such races, the Gran Premio Bari, where sections of the town's streets were closed to make the course.

Without the funding to promote Formula 1 racing in 1956, Bari held its ninth event with two sports-car races, one for under 2-liter cars

ASTON MARTIN DBR1

Relaxed rules for 1957 allowed unlimited prototypes at LeMans and two 3-liter DBR1s and a 3.7-liter DBR2, like this one, were on the starting grid of 54 starters.

Throughout the 1950s, Aston Martins seemed to always run with a power disadvantage against competitors. Even though early engines were of 2.5-liter capacity and were later enlarged to 3 liters, they were still not large or powerful enough in long-distance events like the Mille Miglia, the Targa Florio, Spa, Nurburgring and LeMans.

David Brown saw victory at LeMans as his ultimate goal, and that took powerful cars. In both the 1954 and '55 events, his DB3S sports/racing cars were strong but second places were his closest hits. In the mid-1950s, Brown's commitment to racing escalated to include the design and development of a new engine for a new car. It took some time, but with John Wyer at the helm of Aston Martin racing, results were finally rewarded.

In 1955, Wyer started two new engine projects: the 3-liter RB6 race engine for the DBR1 race car and the 3.7-liter DB4 engine for the production sports car.

Ted Cutting took on the RB6 project. This all-aluminum engine featured a bore and stroke of 83 X 90mm and used the same twin-plug head with 60° valve angles used in the DB3S. Later, Cutting revised the head with a 95° included valve angle for improved breathing. That produced a winning power plant.

The DB4 engine project was tackled by Tadek Marek, a Polish-born engineer. This 92 X 92mm engine later became the basis of the DBR2 race car.

The DB3S had done its duty well, but escalating demands in international racing replaced it with the DBR1. Its chassis changed from large-diameter tubes in a ladder configuration to small-diameter tubes making a space frame. A five-speed gearbox was incorporated in the ZF final drive for improved weight balance, and the DBR1s were both lower and lighter than the DB3S. When FIA rule changes for 1958 placed a 3-liter limit on engine size, Aston Martin was at last on an equal footing with the competition.

Two early second-place finishes and a convincing 1-2 win at Spa

Aston Martin's greatest win was by Roy Salvadori and Carroll Shelby who drove their DBR1 to victory in the 24-Hours of LeMans, 1959. Shown here at a recent SVRA vintage race in a DBR2, the pair were at it again.

Although the cars looked very similar, the DBR1 and DBR2 were quite different with different chassis designs and power train. The DBR2 engine displaced 3670cc from a bore and stroke of 92 X 92mm. Output in LeMans tune was 287 HP at 5750 rpm versus 255 from the 2992cc DBR1. The DBR2 single-plug head had valves inclined at 80° while the DBR1 dual-plug design began at 60° and was later revised to 95°.

brought the new car laurels in 1957. But its most convincing early win was in the Nurburgring 1000Km where F1 driver Tony Brooks and Noel Cunningham-Reid paced the race from the start and trounced everything, showing that the DBR1 was the better of both Jaguar and Ferrari. Following those thrilling finishes, Tony Brooks won at Spa in a DBR1,

ASTON MARTIN DBR1
1959

2992cc/183-CID DOHC twin-plug in-line 6-cylinder
255 HP @ 6000 rpm
5-speed transaxle
1760 lb, aluminum body w/tubular spaceframe chassis
independent torsion-bar front suspension
de Dion rear axle

and Roy Salvadori won Silverstone in a new DBR2 with a 3.7-liter engine.

Forty-four laps around the demanding 14-mile Nurburgring circuit often brought out the weaknesses of any car. But if there was any doubt about the DBR1's ability, Stirling Moss and Jack Brabham dispelled them with a repeat victory at the 'Ring the following year. Then, in 1959, a single DBR1 was entered for Moss and Jack Fairman who capped off a three-in-a-row win streak at the 'Ring, an important record for Aston Martin.

Race average speed climbed each year from 82.39 mph in 1957 to 84.36 mph in '58, then 85.52 in '59, faster than the following year's Tipo 61 Maserati driven by Moss and Dan Gurney at 82.77 mph for 1000 kilometers.

While the cars raced, further developments at AM produced the DBR2. The DBR2 featured a new competition head with more-radical gear-driven cams, larger valves and a higher compression ratio, 9.3:1. The new car, with Moss driving, took Goodwood, the British Empire

Derived from the 2-liter AC Ace roadster, considerable strengthening was required of the Ace chassis to handle more than double the torque and horsepower of the Ford 4.7-liter 289. The result was a truly sensational roadster, the best performing sports car in the world for the money. List price: $4,800.

were many differences—all with racing in mind.

The first production Cobra, given serial number CSX2000, was shipped from England in early February, 1962. CSX stood for "Carroll Shelby Export" and with that first car came the beginning of a lasting legend of racing. The car was received without engine or transmission, and Shelby and Dean Moon (of the "Moon Equipped" performance-parts fame) soon had a 260-CID high-performance engine and a Borg Warner four-speed installed.

Shelby, the promoter, took over and soon there was a line of people interested in his car. There was just that one car to begin with, but repainting it different colors for each magazine road test made it appear that Cobras were rolling off the assembly line by the dozens. By mid-

May, 1962, two more Cobras built to Shelby's specifications were shipped over from AC for installation of engine and transmission and final prepping for sale. The third Cobra was the first racing Cobra.

The first 75 Cobras built were powered by the HiPo 260. The following 579 received the famed HiPo 289 turning out 271 HP in factory tune. All sorts of in-production changes were incorporated in the cars, including prototypes with Ford's huge NASCAR 427 wedge engine. All totaled, 29 factory-team cars were built along with 11 factory-prepared competition cars in various configurations, ranging from international racing at LeMans to the United States Road Racing Championship (USRRC) series.

In racing tune, Ford's 289 fitted with downdraft Webers cranked out 385 HP and placed the Cobra in the performance league with the best production-class sports/racing cars in the world. Corvettes were no match for these Cobras, which were about 1000 pounds lighter. Chevrolet fans saw their racing fortunes blow away in the dust from Cobras.

A vast list of racing options was offered by Shelby's works and updates were added as soon as they were developed. Thus, independent Cobra racers had support but through 1965, they had to compete against factory cars that left very little worth winning.

One win that Shelby was after was over Ferrari GT cars at LeMans. Two AC Cobras were entered in that 1963 enduro and came away with a rather surprising seventh overall and the 5-liter class victory, averaging 107.99 mph for 2591.83 miles, but behind a Ferrari GTO in second. This AC Cobra was the highest finish of a British entry that year, and showed that Shelby was onto something big. The following year, an American entry factory Cobra with Dan Gurney and Bob Bondurant driving won the 5-liter class again and finished fourth overall. Their pace in a Daytona Coupe Cobra was a healthy 116.30 mph for 2791.24 miles to finish 13 miles ahead of an arch-rival Ferrari GTO whose production quantities never qualified it for GT racing anyway.

Although in manufacture only since 1962, Shelby's Cobra was having an impact on international racing. Ferrari had held World Manufacturer's Championship laurels for years, but the slick-bodied Daytona Coupes came within a whisker of beating the famed Italian cars in 1964, then returned overwhelmingly in 1965 to win America's only World Manufacturer's Championship.

Shelby's 289-CID Cobras also dominated SCCA A/Production and USRRC production-class racing in 1963 and '64, then were surpassed by the absolutely awesome 427 Cobra in 1965.

CARROLL SHELBY

"My idea was to build a car that would outrun the Corvette and Ferrari production cars. Corvettes weighed around 3500 pounds, and Ferrari was sitting around lying, because he would build two or three cars a year like the ones he raced and then say he had built 100 and sign the papers off that he had. I had decided I wanted a car the size of the Austin Healey weighing 2000 or 2500 pounds, with the 221-CID engine.

"So, I wrote to Ford and said I had this chassis, which I didn't. It was only some drawings and sketches, and Don Frey at Ford sent word for me to come in and talk about it. About two days before we were due to meet, I did some projections and figured what it would cost to build a chassis and a body. We saw we'd never be able to do it. So, I called the AC Bristol people to see if they were interested in adapting the AC chassis. They did, Don was interested and that started the Cobra. We built approximately 200 a year.

"We over-engineered the Cobra on purpose. We knew everybody'd be hopping them up and we wanted it for racing anyway. After that first championship, Ford got very interested when they saw we could beat the Corvettes, and they began talking about going to Europe.

"The Daytona Coupe was the thing that really got the Cobra off the ground, as far as international racing was concerned. Without it, we never would have been successful.

"We learned that Corvette was putting a 427 cubic-inch engine in their car, and that presented a problem. Our real aim was to blow the doors off Corvettes, and Ford had 427 fever, too. From the time we thought of the 427 Cobra until the time the first one was running in the States was exactly three months, which shows you what a little company can do when it makes up its mind."

Winner of the LeMans 24-Hour of 1959 with Roy Salvadori in an Aston Martin DBR1.

SCCA national driving champion in 1956 and 1957. USAC national road racing driving champion, 1960.

SPORTS ILLUSTRATED's "Sports Car Driver of the Year," 1956 and 1957.

NEW YORK TIMES "Sportscar Driver of the Year," 1957—58.

Shelby Cobra won the 1965 World Manufacturer's Championship, unseating Ferrari.

Shelby team GT-40 Fords won the 24-Hours of LeMans of 1966 with a 1-2-3 sweep.

Shelby team Mk IV Ford won the 24-Hours of LeMans of 1967, setting distance and average speed records not broken until 1971.

"I didn't actually start getting interested in sports cars until about 1949 or '50. I fell in love with a Jag 120 from the first picture I ever saw of one. Finally got one in 1951, and I started racing in local races around there the same year.

"I tried my hand at trucking and the ready-mix cement business, then I roughnecked in an oilfield. But I couldn't find anything I wanted to do. Finally I went into the chicken business and I really enjoyed that until the price of chicken went straight to hell. So that's when I decided, that well, I'd always wanted to be a race driver.

"We raced an Allard in Argentina where all the Ferraris broke down. That Allard kept going with fenders blowing off and every other damn thing going wrong. We even had a fire in the pits and we didn't have any water, so we smothered it as best we could and finally, Dale Duncan peed down the carburetor. Damned if we didn't end up winning the thing for the United States. I met John Wyer there, who was with Aston Martin at the time, and that's really where I got started.

"As for the idea of the Cobra, I guess that started when Ed Wilkens and I built and raced a flathead Ford special. I decided right then that it was stupid to have expensive foreign cars when you could put an American V8 in easy enough. Ray Brock, then editor of Hot Rod magazine, told me about Ford's new 221 cubic-inch engine.

"Of course, all the time I was driving I never had any money; besides, everybody laughed about my ideas. All the time I was driving in Europe for Wyer I talked about how much I'd like to build a car combining the best of the two worlds.

CORVETTE GRAND SPORT

Zora Arkus-Duntov and others of racing interest at Chevrolet contrived an answer to the Cobra, the Grand Sport Corvette. A total of 125 of these special Corvettes were planned for qualification as GT production cars, but GM's front office canned the project after only three were built and raced.

Carroll Shelby's Cobras were a painful thorn in the pride of Corvette racers. After years of supremacy in SCCA racing, the prospects of being beaten by a Ford-powered sports car was the ultimate indignation for die-hard Chevrolet fans. Their beloved fiberglass two-seaters were finding the going very tough against Shelby's aluminum-bodied roadsters. Nearly 1000 pounds heavier, the 'Vettes were far less nimble than the Cobras, and even though of comparable power combined with a much more-modern chassis, their excess weight kept them on the sidelines of the winner's circle while the Cobras got the wins and attention.

The solution? Another Corvette, one specially designed and built for racing with all the right stuff and a lot less weight. As stories began circulating about the new cars in late 1962, interest in Corvette's return to supremacy was encouraging to racers and fans alike. But, the cars didn't materialize quite as planned.

The General Motors front office was the problem. Regardless of the prestige Chevrolet stood to gain from being #1 on race day, management continued its stance of no factory racing as accepted under the AMA ban. It was a frustrating time for Corvette racing, because it appeared that all efforts were shot in the foot by GM's own management.

Grand Sports styling mirrored production Sting Ray Corvettes, but that's where the similarity stopped. With attention paid to weight reduction, the Grand Sports were some 1350-lb lighter than showroom Corvettes.

Early Grand Sports like this third one built ran aluminum 327-based small-block engines. It is now fitted with a 427 incher prepped for full-bore racing. In Grand Sport form, aluminum 377-CID small-blocks were said to have the capability of 550 HP with fuel injection.

And, even though privateers tried their best, Cobra and Ford were the big names in SCCA production-class sports-car racing.

Hope for the return of Corvette was seen in Chevrolet Division's new boss, Semon (Bunkie) Knudsen. He became Chevrolet general manager following an illustrious stint in the same post at Pontiac. Under his direction, the staid old Indian became a highly regarded warrior in the late 1950s, and Knudsen's philosophy carried on with the GTO and other performance Pontiacs after his departure to Chevrolet where he gave the go-ahead for a variety of performance-oriented Chevrolets.

One was a new Corvette. SCCA regulations specified that a minimum of 100 cars had be built to qualify as production-class cars. The Grand Sport was Duntov's solution to the Cobra-Corvette problem and he planned to produce 125. That generated considerable excitement as fans couldn't wait to see the cars in winning action. Then the specter of the AMA ban rose again in early 1963 when GM management restated its acceptance of the earlier ruling.

The Grand Sport project stopped after only five were completed. These cars were another of Duntov's pet projects and his able direction saw them come in at under 1900 pounds. All 125 would have amounted to a mere drop in Chevrolet's corporate bucket, and in SCCA and FIA racing, they were certain to receive wide international attention. From FIA, the European rules committee responded to inquiries about homologation that the Grand Sports would be recognized after only a few were built if Chevrolet acted in good faith and produced the required minimum number. LeMans 1963 was the Grand Sport's planned European debut, but the required number was not built and the Grand Sports were not on the starting grid.

However, the early Grand Sports showed brilliantly at times but were always outclassed by the front-engine Chaparral and Scarab, and

rear-engine Lotus 23B and Porsche RS-60 Spyders they were pitted against. In testing at Sebring, Masten Gregory is said to have lapped a Grand Sport under the record set in 1961 by Stirling Moss' Birdcage Maserati.

The first three Grand Sports were powered by Chevrolet's famed aluminum-alloy small-block V8, taken to 377 cubic inches, that turned out 480 HP. Except for fearsome styling beyond the normal Sting Ray and wide Halibrand racing wheels with fat tires, most components were production Corvette items.

The Grand Sports were raced sporadically by independents and put on an exciting show at Nassau during the Speed Week of 1963. Three of them were among the Mecom-Chevrolet Racing Team. They finished fourth and eighth in the 232-mile Nassau Trophy race after making unscheduled pit stops. Neither finished the Tourist Trophy race because of rear-axle failure, but returned with improvements in the 112-mile Governor's Cup race where Roger Penske and Augie Pabst finished third and fourth behind two prototypes.

CORVETTE GRAND SPORT
1963

6180cc/377-CID aluminum Chevrolet V8
480 HP @ 6000 rpm
4-speed transmission
1900 lb, fiberglass body w/ladder-type tubular-steel frame
4-wheel independent suspension

When the Grand Sports ran wheel to wheel with Cobras, they exhibited a margin of superiority that showed them to be both faster and better handlers. However, Cobras were production cars and the Grand Sports were not, an important distinction.

Roger Penske returned to the Bahamas Speed Week and won the Nassau Trophy race of 1964. It would be more or less the swan song of the Grand Sport Corvette saga. The last two cars appeared in 1965, one with Chevrolet's new 427-CID big-block engine and the other as Targa roadster with sidedraft Weber carburetors on a 327-CID small-block. Although larger and heavier than the 327, the fantastic torque of the 427 produced an even more-awesome car.

Unfortunately, the 427-CID Grand Sport Corvette was at best a last effort in a rapidly changing world of racing. Carroll Shelby had just introduced his updated version of the Cobra with a highly advanced coil-spring chassis and Ford's well-proven 427-CID engine. Thus, the new 427 Cobra became another pain in the pride of Corvette racers.

The new Cobras were raced by independents and returned five more A/Production championships to become one of the most highly regarded sports cars of modern times. In contrast, Chevrolet claimed not to be involved in racing, and thus capped the Grand Sport Corvette.

Although Duntov's efforts amounted to a tiny expense to GM, management always seemed to spoil the fun. Thus, the Grand Sports are not well known but no doubt remain the ultimate mid-'60s Corvettes.

CHEETAH

The Cheetah was a truly aggressive design with immense appeal as an extremely fast sports/racing car. Rough around the edges, Cheetahs suffered from blistering cockpit heat.

The early 1960s was a time when the public's interest in sports-car racing came on strong, and both the Cobra and Cheetah were signs of those times. Bill Thomas' Cheetah was his all-American answer to the Cobra, a very quick and fast answer. It was also another a good idea for Chevrolet racing that went largely ignored.

Before the Cobra in 1963, private-entry Corvettes were dominant in SCCA production sports-car racing. Thomas was squarely in the middle of it all with a record of wins that earned him the widely respected title of "Mr. Corvette." Based in California, Thomas built a variety of cars that were highly successful in road and drag racing. He, too, enjoyed the successes of Chevrolet racing and prepared cars that won more than 100 races five seasons in a row. One of his 'Vettes won all

but two of 56 races entered! He could tweak small-blocks to over 500 HP, and knowing how to get extra juice from Chevrolet's Rochester fuel-injection systems was his specialty.

But Corvette National Championships stopped when the Cobras showed up. Shelby ripped through the Corvettes, leaving little of consequence, and the Chevy crowd shook their heads in disbelief. Thomas saw what was happening and returned to his shop to counter the Cobras with an all-new racer, a lightweight and powerful car of modern design—the Cheetah.

Legend has it that Thomas and Chevrolet Division's Ed Cole struck a secret deal to produce 100 Cheetahs in order to qualify as production cars. Their target was SCCA A/Production and their intended victims were Shelby and his Cobras. The reason for secrecy was that GM management had reinforced its 1957 Automobile Manufacturer's Association edict against factory involvement in racing during February, 1963. That

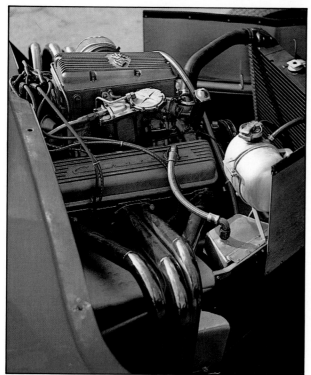

Austere, simple, functional; everything needed to go very fast very quickly. Exceptional handling, excellent braking and phenomenal acceleration were the performance features of the Bill Thomas Cheetah.

Tricks that Bill Thomas had developed earned him the respected title of "Mr. Corvette". His Cheetah also benefitted from that know-how. He tweaked Chevy's 327-CID small-block to 377-CID and increased output to 520 HP on Rochester fuel injection.

ended Chevrolet Division's ultra-lightweight Corvette Grand Sport project. Although GM chose not to compete against its customers, Chevrolet quietly supplied selected teams with all sorts of the latest goodies—for engineering testing purposes—and factory engineers regularly attended races on "vacation."

The Cheetah was a different sort of problem, though. A few teams with two or three cars for NASCAR or road racing or drag racing was one thing, but producing 100 sports cars in 12 months was beyond the capacity of normal racing efforts and required extensive facilities. Yet, Thomas went to work to do just that in an effort to have a Chevrolet competitor against Ford's sponsorship of Shelby's Cobras.

Zora Arkas-Duntov and Bill Mitchell at Chevrolet Division were in a far better position to produce the required number of cars. They planned to build 125 Grand Sport Corvettes, but the ban stopped that after only five were completed. With his connections and previous Corvette successes, Thomas could provide Chevrolet with an alternative

sports car to keep Cobras out of the winner's circle.

The Grand Sports raced a few times while "on loan" and clearly showed their potential, about 9 seconds a lap faster than Cobras at Nassau, but the Cheetah was simply in a higher league, an astounding performer. Thomas and Don Edmunds laid out the car on a front-engine/rear-drive configuration with the engine set well back in a mid-chassis position. The coupe body style with its gullwing doors stands to this day as one of the most aggressive automotive designs ever.

The cockpit sat over the rear wheels with interior space tight but with all the essentials for blasting any Cobra in sight. On a 90-inch wheelbase, the engine/transmission assembly sat so far back that the output shaft of its Corvette aluminum four-speed transmission coupled to the rear end with only one universal joint. The rear suspension was a modified '63 Corvette and many heavy-duty Chevy components completed the lightweight, but durable, sports cars. Its tubular semi-space-frame chassis was fitted with Thomas' famous 327-CID engine taken up to 377 cubic inches, running Rochester fuel injection.

Weighing in at 1510 pounds, a Cheetah was a full 500 pounds lighter than a Cobra, and when dynoed at 520 HP, it had a 140-HP margin. The chassis design gave lateral acceleration of 1.18g, far better than a Corvette, and placed the Cheetah in the performance league of rear-engine Chaparrals, Lolas and King Cobras, but not the Cobra roadsters as planned.

The Cheetah/Cobra duel never happened. Only 27 Cheetahs were built according to one counting and as few as 13 by another. Regardless of their numbers, Cheetahs were blindingly fast, but raced in prototype classes against rear-engine prototypes.

The first two Cheetahs received aluminum bodies while all others got fiberglass. Like all new racing cars, development problems had to be solved, but one never cured was cockpit heat. Cheetahs were like ovens. Each interior footbox was located beside the engine with the top and outboard sides very close to the header tubes. Thus, cockpit heating was intense.

CHEETAH
1964

6180cc/377-CID aluminum Chevrolet V8
520 HP @ 7000 rpm
Chevrolet 4-speed transmission
1510 lb, fiberglass body w/tubular semi-spaceframe chassis
4-wheel independent suspension

Nevertheless, Jerry Grant of Seattle, Washington, and both Ralph Salyer and Bud Clusserath from Hammond, Indiana, raced the cars very effectively. Salyer set a blazing top speed of 215 mph on Daytona's high banks, whereupon the body disintegrated. He also won the June Sprints at Elkhart Lake in both 1964 and '65. His top speed there in '64 was a highly disputed 185 mph, but the next year he did the same to quell disbelievers of his Cheetah's performance potential.

A Cheetah topped 198 mph at Riverside against rear-engine prototypes, the beginnings of Can-Am style racing, where Grant was faster than Shelby American's top driver, Ken Miles, in a Cobra-powered Cooper Monaco that became known as the King Cobra. Cheetahs won 11 C-Sports/Modified class races that year, 1964, and finished Riverside's end-of-season race second overall.

Thomas was also a highly successful drag racer in his Cheetah.

Bill Thomas tried to do for Chevrolet what Shelby did for Ford. But like other sports cars before it, Thomas' Cheetah was ignored by GM even though Chevrolet stood to gain immense prestige with a sports car of its type. Cheetahs exceeded 185 mph in sports-car races and won against stiff competition, but never raced in GT class against Cobras.

Consistent 1/4-mile stats were low 10s at around 135 mph.

In an effort to increase production, Thomas planned to build Super Cheetahs for the street. Unfortunately, his shop burned and ended all hope of building 100 cars. No one at GM could provide needed support because of corporate handcuffs, and Thomas's offer for Chevrolet racing passed into sports-car history, having never competed against Cobras.

The Cheetah's mark in history was fantastic acceleration, phenomenal cornering and truly awesome overall performance, a better idea that Chevrolet let slip away as the record books filled with Ford.

125

COBRA DAYTONA COUPE

Designed and developed by Pete Brock and Phil Remington with considerable input from Ken Miles and Carroll Shelby, the Cobra Daytona Coupe was first raced at Daytona 1964, thus the origin of its name. It succeeded in beating the Ferrari GTO to win the World Manufacturer's Championship in 1965. Photo by Bob D'Olivo courtesy of Petersen Publishing Co.

To almost everyone, a Cobra is a roadster. But for a few enthusiasts up on their cars, the Cobra coupes are an enduring success story, one that began in September, 1963, and became America's only World Manufacturer's Champion on July 4, 1965, just 22 months later.

Recalling that GT racing at the time was almost exclusively the domain of Ferrari, it is intriguing to note that the Cobra coupe was a quest by a small group of dedicated Shelby American men to unseat the famed Italian cars. Their goal was to design and build a slick coupe for the Cobra's rather dated chassis to challenge the might of Ferrari's tradition.

While Ford Motor Co. was applying dollars and resources to its GT-40 project, Shelby American went after Ferrari GT cars largely on its own. Ferrari had vast experience with the V12 250 GT series of cars while Shelby American was barely one-year old when the coupe project began. Although the roadsters proved to be SCCA championship cars, the coupe design team recognized that those high-powered "bricks," in

terms of aerodynamics, would have to be more sophisticated in shape.

FIA regulations allowed coupe bodies as long as they were built on production chassis and drive lines. With that incentive, team-leader Pete Brock, Phil Remington from Lance Reventlow's Scarab organization, and test-driver Ken Miles set to producing the first Cobra coupe for debut at Daytona, 1963. By the time the project was in full swing, there was barely three months to have the car ready.

In mid-stream, an aerodynamicist calculated that Brock's design would take 450 HP to go 160 mph. In other words, his seat-of-the-pants approach was calculated to be a failure. But when first tested at Riverside, Miles tagged 165 the first time out. So much for theory.

Compared to the Ferrari 250 GTO it was destined to race against, the coupe body was 10-mph slower in top speed. To compensate, the Cobra V8's excellent low-end torque gave it sensational pulling power out of turns and actually resulted in better lap times. The well-proven Weber-equipped 289-CID Cobra engine turned out 385 HP and, as expected, it went faster than the roadster with the added plus of using 25 percent less fuel. Thus, it was a definite threat to the GTO.

The Daytona Continental 24-Hour of 1963 saw the debut of the first Cobra coupe, chassis number CSX2287. In the eighth hour, the car was

Stark! Just the bare necessities to win international races. Dan Gurney and Bob Bondurant finished fourth overall at LeMans 1964 by averaging 116.30 mph for 2791.24 miles, a new GT distance record. Photo by Bob D'Olivo courtesy of Petersen Publishing Co.

Based on Ford's production cast-iron 289-CID engine, the Cobra engine was bumped to 385 HP at 7000 rpm. Cobra's racing successes are all the more impressive considering the level of sophistication found in the competition, most notably the Ferrari SOHC V12. Photo by Bob D'Olivo courtesy of Petersen Publishing Co.

leading overall with a lap record of 2:08.2 minutes at 106.99 mph average. Then, fate struck during a pit stop when spilled fuel splashed on the car's overheated differential and burst into flames. Although doused in time to save the car, it was sidelined. But it returned to action at Sebring where it had become known as the Cobra Daytona Coupe.

Sebring was its first taste of victory, a resounding upset of both Ferrari and Texas oilman John Mecom's Grand Sport Corvettes. Dave McDonald and Bob Holbert finished fourth overall ahead of two Cobra roadsters in at fifth and sixth. Finishing 209 laps, the Daytona Coupe averaged 90.57 mph during the 12 hours, just 2.16 mph off the pace of the winning Parkes/Maglioli Ferrari 275 P prototype.

The Daytona Coupe raced first in Europe at Spa, Belgium for the 500 Km where Phil Hill set a GT lap record of 4:04.5 minutes at 129.01 mph. However, clogged fuel filters held back the car for another Ferrari win. Readied for LeMans, an additional Daytona Coupe made up a three-car team. After the first one, all subsequent coupes were bodied by Carrozzeria Grand Sport of Modena, Italy. Pete Brock's small team was not able to body the cars in time, and Alessandro De Tomaso referred his long-time-friend Shelby to the Italian coach builders.

Shelby's works built the chassis and sent them to Italy for bodies. A fortuitous error of a two-inch, too-high cowl subframe in one of the cars produced one coupe with two-inches more head room. When Dan Gurney became a Shelby team driver, this was the only coupe he could fit in. It thus became his car, CSX2299. He and Bob Bondurant brought the car in at fourth overall at LeMans, 1964, to post a highly acclaimed defeat of Ferrari's GTO. Their GT class victory of 116.30 mph for 24-hours and 2791.24 miles showed the Daytona Coupes more than met the Ferrari challenge.

But, the season was not over. Ferrari won at Reims, then Gurney won the RAC Tourist Trophy. The following Monza 1000 Km was canceled when FIA and the Italian race organizers argued over the homologation of the Ferrari 250 LM. FIA did not accept the rear-engine cars as production GT cars and the organizers wanted it so. Thus, without Monza, the Tour de France and Bridgehampton became very important. Ferrari's experience shown in the Tour and the Cobra roadsters swept Bridgehampton, but the Italian cars squeaked by for another World Manufacturer's Champion, 84.6 points to 78.3.

The following year was a different story. Five coupes had been finished and spent the winter in preparation for the 1965 season. They finished 2-4-6 overall at Daytona with a class win. Sebring saw them sweep the top four GT positions followed by the top two GT spots in the Monza 1000 Km. No Cobras appeared in the Targa Florio and Ferrari won in Sicily, but it was clear that the Daytona coupes were superior to the 250 GTO. Ferrari recognized that by retiring his factory-team cars.

Then, at Spa, a private-entry GTO showed its heels to the Cobras for the GT points. Next, Bondurant set the absolute GT record at Nurburgring where the Daytona Coupes won their class in first, second and third. Along with a host of Fords, the Daytona Coupes then entered the LeMans 24-Hours, but searing heat took its toll on the cars with only a single Cobra finishing, eighth overall. But, the durability of the Ferraris showed very well, a 1-2-3 overall sweep and GT-class points.

Following the June debacle at LeMans, Shelby sent his coupes to Reims for the July 4th 12-hour contest. It was in that French event that the efforts of Brock, Remington, Miles and the Daytona Coupe team attained the highest glory, the World Manufacturer's Championship. Drivers Bondurant and Jo Schlesser teamed to cap Carroll Shelby's quest to offer the public a fast sports car and to beat Ferrari with it.

The Daytona Coupes succeeded where no other American marque had before. Shelby built a total of 654 Cobras from 1962 through mid-1965, including the six coupes, with funding drawn largely from the sales base of Shelby American cars sold through Ford dealers. Ford Motor Company backed his operation and provided management support to ensure profitability, and Shell Oil Co. provided some support for racing. But his Cobras were largely his team's own products, a great credit to tireless dedication where a few young and dynamic people took on the greatest marque of their time and changed the course of racing history.

COBRA DAYTONA COUPE
1964

4738cc/289-CID cast-iron Ford V8
385 HP @ 7000 rpm
Ford 4-speed transmission
1950 lb, aluminum body w/tubular frame
4-wheel independent suspension with transverse leaf springs

BOB BONDURANT

"I started racing in 1956 in a Morgan Plus-4. After that I drove an Austin-Healey and from that into a modified Triumph, bored and stroked with a locked-up rear end. I ran against Maserati and Ferrari 3-liter cars and won quite a few west-coast races in that car, believe it or not.

"Then I went to Europe for Shelby in 1964 and '65 in the Ford Cobras and campaigned the Daytona Coupes against Ferrari. We won the World Manufacturer's Championship in 1965, and I stayed over there after that

and drove for Ferrari and Porsche in some long-distance races.

"I also drove Formula 1 in 1966. My first Ferrari ride was a V6 Dino 206S at Monza, where I crashed in practice. After that, I drove a BRM Formula 1. Rindt and I drove a 250 LM to ninth at Daytona, and Paul Hawkins and I finished fourth at Nurburgring '66 in a Porsche 906.

"My transition to big-time driving occurred when I went to Europe with the Cobras. We beat Ferrari in '65, the first time it had happened in five years. That was an accomplishment the whole team felt really good about.

"I drove the Cobra FIA roadsters and Daytona Coupes for Shelby along with the GT-40s. My first race in a GT-40 was in the Daytona Continental 24-Hour in '65 where Ritchie Ginther and I finished third behind two other Shelby team cars. I raced both the GT-40 and Cobras that year, the GT-40 at LeMans.

"The year before, Dan Gurney and I won the GT class and fourth overall at LeMans in a Daytona Coupe, my first year in the 24-Hours. That was really exciting, my first really big success. In '65, Jo Schlesser and I won the GT class in one at Sebring, another overall, then Alan Grant and I finished eighth in the Monza 1000 Km. Neerspach and I drove to a seventh at Nurburgring. Each final was a win in GT.

"At the end of each season, I came back to the United States and drove what became Cooper Can-Am cars. In '67, I drove the USRRC and was going to drive Can-Am, but I had a bad crash in a McLaren Mk II. The steering broke at Watkins Glen coming out of a corner at 150 mph. I went sideways, then end-over-end eight times and broke my legs, ribs, ankles and a few other things.

"While recovering in bed, I was thinking what to do next. I looked over the schools in Europe and thought I'd like to put my knowledge into one here. That was almost 20 years ago now, and my school is still going strong. I really love it, and I still race a little from time to time, like vintage racing. It's lots of fun."

Valvoline's "Best Corvette Drive of the Year", 1959.

1959 SCCA B-Production Championship.

128

CHAPARRAL-2

Designed, developed and driven by Hall and Hap Sharp, shown here at Sebring during the 20th anniversary of the Sebring win, the Chaparral-2 was the leading edge of new racing technology in its day. Its fiberglass monocoque chassis and automatic transmission are just two examples.

The view seen most often by competitors of the Chaparral-2 cars. Lola and McLaren were to later succeed in building Can-Am championship cars.

In the annals of Chevy-powered road racing, there is only one marque of all-American designed and powered, all-American driven racing cars that challenged the Europeans in endurance racing and won on their own turf. The marque is Chaparral, and the man behind them was Jim Hall. His Chevrolet-powered cars rank as America's premier prototype racing cars of the 1960s.

Hall began racing in the early 1950s, then went off to the California Institute of Technology to become a mechanical engineer. Both efforts proved to be the roots for creating legends as his experience at the wheels of world-class cars of the time honed his driving talents. When he recognized that the availability of parts for leading European racing cars was a continual problem, he decided to design and build his own cars.

After a season of racing in Europe, it was clear that he could do just as well at designing and building racing cars as his European contemporaries. The top cars of 1960 were rear-engine Coopers and Lotus

Another application of Chevrolet's aluminum 327 V8 produced a very reliable 420 HP at 6500 rpm on Webers. These cars were guarded with secrecy and generally regarded as a Chevrolet "back-door" racing program.

formula racers, and they inspired Hall to create his own rear-engine sports/racing car. But his first effort was with a more-conventional design, a front-engine car designed and built by the team of Troutman and Barnes in California.

Their experience with sports cars came from building Lance Reventlow's Scarabs of the late '50s. Built for Hall, the first Chaparrals were similar to Scarabs: small, lightweight, tubular-frame with a front-engine layout. Power for the Chaparrals came from a Corvette small-bock engine stroked to 318 cubic inches. Rated about 325 HP at 6500 rpm, these 1480-pound Class B racers promised to be formidable competitors but didn't produce the overall results Hall wanted.

After the six Troutman and Barnes Chaparrals, Hall undertook to design, build and race his own cars. He and Hap Sharp worked out the plan, then proceeded to build the Chaparral-2 in Hall's Midland, Texas, shop. These cars were very different from the aluminum-bodied Troutman and Barnes cars. Starting with a fiberglass monocoque chassis, not steel as in the GT-40 or aluminum as in other cars, Hall produced an advanced design in 1963 that foretold the coming of Can-Am cars of similar design.

A Ford GT-40 had won the Daytona Continental 24-Hour that year, so the challenge came from Ferrari, world champions at the time, and Ford whose megabuck GT-40s were on the move to unseat Ferrari. Jim Hall's small racing team faced both formidable opponents and, nevertheless, led by a sizable margin in torrential rains that filled up the cockpit. Hap Sharp drove through most of the rain, and Hall took the checkered flag. That proved the all-American Chaparral-2, the car shown here with Hap Sharp at the wheel, to be more than a match for the best racing cars in the world.

This model Chaparral-2 was the most successful car Hall and Sharp built. There were big wins with later cars—the '66 Nurburgring 1000 Km in a 2D, the '67 BOAC 500 at Brands Hatch with a 2F and others—but Sebring was the biggest for Hall.

Automatic transmissions in their various forms were a significant factor in the success of the Chaparrals, especially against the likes of Ford, which experimented with them but couldn't get them to work in their GT-40s and went back to four-speed manuals.

Thus, the all-American Chaparral-2 with Chevy power proved its worth in full-bore competition from sprint-type racing that later became the Can-Am series, and in international endurance racing at Sebring. Jim Hall's genius at designing and building world-class racing cars combined with his driving talent also proved the worth of Chevrolet's small-block engine, a true racing workhorse in its own right. Together, they challenged the best racing cars and drivers in the world and won.

CHAPARRAL-2
1964

5360cc/327-CID aluminum Chevrolet V8
420 HP @ 6500 rpm
automatic transmission
1740 lb, fiberglass monocoque body/chassis
all independent suspension

One advance was automatic transmission, an idea first proposed by Hap Sharp. In the Chaparral-2 form, it was a two-speed dog-clutch unit with a torque converter said to have "two gears"—fast and faster! Raced under a shroud of secrecy, there was much controversy surrounding that transmission, fueling speculation that the Chaparral-2s were really built by Chevrolet and handed out the back door to Hall.

Not so says Hall. Although there was a close relationship between his concern, Chaparral Cars, and Chevrolet engineering people who were also concerned about vehicle dynamics, Hall says the cars were developed and built by his group of about eight people. Even the form of the fiberglass body was made by Hall and his wife, Sandy, who shaped the clay for the molds. Bodies were made in Fort Worth, Texas, by Andy Green.

First raced in 1963, the Chaparral-2 was the first in the line of Chaparrals that included the 2C and 2D coupes for endurance racing, open 2E Can-Am cars with a wing, 2F endurance coupes, open 2G Can-Am cars, the unsuccessful 2H and the last Chaparral sports-racing car, the 2J ground-effects "sucker car." In total, perhaps 20 Chaparral-2 cars were built and Hall owns them all.

Beginning the line was the Hall/Sharp team of white cars carrying numbers 65 and 66. Powered by aluminum-block 327-CID small-blocks and fed by Webers, they dominated the pro-racing circuit by winning 16 of 21 races entered. These 1650-pound cars with around 420 HP were the top American racing cars of their time, and their biggest win came at Sebring, 1965 against Europe's best.

JIM HALL

Art Eastman photo.

"I started driving racing cars when I was in college, and then got interested in what makes a car go and handle, probably because of driving. I graduated with a mechanical engineering degree, but didn't apply it for quite a while.

"Back then, we were just amateur racers out having fun, and when a car didn't handle right, we complained about it. Later on we were doing some pretty good racing in this country and got to see Europe's top drivers and cars at Nassau and Sebring. But when you wanted to buy one of the latest cars from a European builder, they wouldn't sell you one because they were running factory teams, and what you got was last year's model if you were lucky.

"Around 1960, I decided that, for the amount of money we were spending, I ought to be able to build a competitive car, and through a long process of learning and lots of good suggestions from Hap Sharp and a lot of other people, I think we did some really outstanding development of racing-car technology and produced a lot of original ideas.

"The Chaparral-2 was one of the most successful cars we have built, including our Indianapolis 500 cars. We won 16 out of 21 races entered in 1965, and for me as a driver, winning Sebring in '65 with the Chaparral-2 was one of my biggest wins.

"We had a five lap lead during the rain when the fastest competitor was running 22 minutes a lap. In the pit, Hap and I had a big discussion about going back out. If the car sat there for an hour, we would still have had the lead, but Hap wanted to go. I gave in and he jumped in the car. His first lap took 20 minutes.

"All the time, we were wondering if he was stuck in a puddle somewhere which would have put us out of the race, but he finally came by at maybe 40 or 50 mph.

"Water was so deep in places that it came in the radiator opening, up over the top of the car and filled up the cockpit. While Hap was out, it had gotten dark, and when he came in, he was cold and wet and ready to get out. But I said I didn't know where the puddles were so he should continue driving. You should have seen the look on his face! But he did it and drove another hour and half, three hours in the rain.

"I drove the last hour of the race, winning by four laps ahead of a GT-40 Ford.

"My favorite win, though, was at Mosport, Canada, in '65 when I started last because of not qualifying due to a failed engine. I worked my way through the pack with the Chaparral-2, passed the leader, Bruce McLaren, on the next to last lap and won the race."

United States Road Racing Champion, 1964

PORSCHE 904

Porsche's remarkable Type 904 had many class wins on many international circuits, the 48th Targa Florio of 1964 for instance where the cars scored a very impressive 1-2.

The final edition of Porsche's long line of famous four-cam racing cars powered by Dr. Fuhrmann's engine was the Type 904. Introduced late in 1963, 904s were all-new with no design ties to the 356 line, although evolution of the spyders contributed to their development. The first six were works cars with the following 100 being identical customer cars.

The 904s were built rapidly, four or five a day, as the requirement of at least 100 was set by FIA and other sanctioning bodies to qualify as production GT cars. In order to meet deadlines, Stuttgart chose a new direction and began contracting major sections of construction to outside shops rather than building them in its own race shop. Heinkel, of aircraft fame, built and wired the 904s which were also Porsche's first complete all-fiberglass-bodied cars.

Design of the 904 was the product of "Butzi" Porsche, head stylist of his grandfather's firm. A product more of intuition than scientific testing, the 904 yielded an excellent drag coefficient of just 0.34 and stood only 42 inches high. They were robust cars with the capacity of running either four-, six- or eight-cylinder engines in a variety of forms, from rally specials to GT and prototype classes. Their first form was to use the four-cylinder GT Carrera engine, although they were also testbeds for development of future models. The 904s proved overwhelmingly successful at outlasting their competition. Their combination of speed, handling and durability proved "Butsi" Porsche's intuition to be on the mark as the 904s became four-cylinder giant-killers.

In four-cylinder form, 1988cc and 198 HP, 904s were priced FOB Stuttgart at $7425 and were another in the line of Porsche's excellent race-ready bargains. Curb weight was about 1350 pounds and top speed was beyond 150 mph with 0—60-mph times of 6.4 seconds. As "Grand

Fuhrmann four-cam reached its zenith with the Type 904. After ten years in use as Porsche's main-line racing engine, the Type 547 had gone through several variations to produce 180 HP at 7000 rpm from 1966cc in 904 GTS race tune.

Like all Porsche's, the interior of the Type 904 offered both sports-car enthusiasts and racing drivers the essentials in a well-rounded two-place GT coupe.

Touring" cars, 904s were stark by comparison to typical road-going GTs of the period, but were designed for road racing where the rules made no distinction between a purpose-built GT class racer and a converted production model.

During the late 1950s and early '60s, International racing regulations changed. Primary emphasis shifted from the '50s-era sports/racing cars, where numbers produced was of no concern, to production sports cars where minimums were set. The Type 904 was a product of the early 1960s and embodied little more than the necessities to race and win. They met all of FIA's GT rules right down to a "luggage" space of 65 X 40 X 20cm.

When introduced, it was quickly realized that the 904 was a leading contender in the 2-liter category of FIA's Constructors Championship on the international level, and also fit SCCA's Manufacturer's Division in the U. S. Road Racing Championship. Production requirements were met quickly as the cars were ordered by leading Porsche teams around the world.

Comparing other 2-liter GT cars of the time at Riverside, the 904 was about four seconds a lap faster than a 1600 Carrera and about nine

seconds faster than an MGB. In 2-liter Modified, where the 904 first ran in USRRC racing, 904s were less dominant and posted times about four seconds off the pace of Lotus 23s with 2-liter Climax engines and were about three seconds behind Lotus 23-Bs with 1.6-liter twin-cam Ford engines.

In U.S. racing, the durability of 904s proved to be a class-winning asset and regularly brought them in just behind AC Cobras whose 4.7-liter (289-CID) V8s produced about 375 HP. What made 904s welcomed by American racers was Porsche's sound engineering, thorough development and support of the cars for successful private-entry racing. The results were SCCA class National Championships in both 1964 and '65.

In Europe, 904s ran all major circuits and immediately emerged as winners. In their first European outing (1964), 904s took a 1-2 in Sicily's grueling Targa Florio, a stunning overall victory for a new GT car. At Nurburgring a third overall and class victory was earned. A seventh at LeMans and the Thermal Index followed, then a class win at Riems, a fifth on Spa's very fast circuit, then a class sweep at Zolder, Belgium, followed by a 2-3 finish in England's legendary Tourist Trophy—

Construction of fiberglass on a boxed steel chassis, the Type 904 was the first such undertaking by Porsche. The result became the ultimate four-cam, four-cylinder racer from Zuffenhausen.

But like the 550, the 904 was rather short lived in comparison to the longevity of the 356. Only during 1964 and '65 were 904s campaigned from the factory.

Both the 550 and variants of the 356 carried the famed four-cam engine as in the 904, the last of the line with that engine. Its origin came from inspired design and determination on the part of Dr. Ernst Fuhrmann to produce a rugged engine capable of obtaining at least 70 HP/liter. Fuhrmann undertook to design the four-cammer, first designated as the Type 547 engine, in 1952 when the Company was only two years old as a Stuttgart manufacturer and resided in a corner of Reutters body shop. The Type 547 was a technically advanced engine for its day; assembly was complicated and required some 120 hours from a skilled assembler.

PORSCHE 904 GTS
1964

1966cc/120-CID DOHC air-cooled flat 4-cylinder
180 HP @ 7000 rpm
5-speed transmission
1825 lb, fiberglass body bonded to pressed-steel frame
4-wheel coil-spring independent suspension

This air-cooled boxer-4 engine was designed around hemispherical combustion chambers and incorporated dry-sump lubrication, twin ignition, dual roller-bearing camshafts per set of cylinders and was fed by dual-throat carburetors. At the time, Porsche Type 356 cars used a 38-HP engine, but the Type 547 engine produced 112 HP from 1.5 liters on the first try. Weighing about 310 pounds dry, the Type 547 went through several evolutions and ultimately approached 200 HP at 7000 rpm from 2 liters in the 904.

The Fuhrmann four-cam engine proved to be Porsche's most-successful masterpiece in the early years and was a mainline powerplant for 12 full seasons of racing. It was also a bold and expensive undertaking for a fledgling automotive manufacturer, yet proved to be the single most-important factor in Porsche's rise as a force to be reckoned with.

By 1966, the Carrera GTS 904s were fielded by privateers as the works cars became the Type 906, a radically different car with a six-cylinder engine. The demands of racing were changing and Porsche had continually grown as a manufacturer to the point that overall wins in such highly acclaimed races as the 24-Hours of LeMans and the World Manufacturer's Championship were becoming distinct possibilities. Thus, the Type 904 was the last of the "old-line" cars from Porsche as a new competition department was formed around a new generation of youthful Porsche people whose objective it was to go for the big ones.

Porsche's best-ever finish there. In the Tour de France, 904s finished 3-4-5-6 behind V12 Ferrari GTOs and 1-2 on handicap. Through 1965, 904s were Porsche's mainline weapon and finished a stunning 4-5 at LeMans '65, winning the 2-liter class, and each car won the Index of Performance and Index of Thermal Efficiency, respectively.

In SCCA racing, Porsche was a co-winner of the Manufacturer's Championship in 1965 along with Carroll Shelby's famed Cobra. Each earned 63 points to tie while Charlie Kolb won the A/Production championship in the Southeast Region in a 904. Cobra won four of the remaining five regions.

Surprisingly, 904s were also superb rally cars and took Porsche honors in a variety of long-distance, all-weather durability runs throughout Europe. Monte Carlo, considered to be the toughest rally test on both cars and drivers, saw a 904 finish a highly acclaimed second overall in 1965 among only 22 finishers in a field of 237 entrants.

Many similar awards in all sorts of competition showed the Type 904 to be a thoroughbred design and proved the concept of a purpose-built racing car to be superior to converting production sports cars for racing. Porsche had shown that philosophy before with the successful 550 Spyder.

ALFA ROMEO GTZ

Alfa Romeo GTZ (Giulia Tubolare Zagato) was the 1964 entry from the famed Italian marque. Very light and responsive, the cars were class winners in all sorts of international races, the 1600cc class at LeMans '64 for instance.

The GTZ name means, Giulia Tubolare Zagato. Giulia is the type name of the Alfa line giving rise to these superb racing cars and Tubolare refers to its tubular frame, while Zagato is well known in coachwork. That's the name, but the purpose was more than a name. The statement was that Alfa Romeo was back into racing. The time was 1964. But first, a little history.

Dominating Grand Prix racing following the second world war was Alfa's first postwar venture. The prewar Alfetta's (little Alfas) were based on the 1.5-liter "Voiturette" class of open-wheel racing. These were the supercharged Tipo 158 and Tipo 159. Rules allowed either 4.5-liter unsupercharged or 1.5-liter supercharged engines, and Alfa just happened to have its 1938-model cars on hand to bring up to regulations for postwar racing.

With the German cars gone during this period, Alfa emerged as the commanding marque. When the 158s were made durable, they were virtually unbeatable. They won three out of four races entered in 1946, then returned the following year to win convincingly with top drivers Achille Varzi and Jean-Pierre Wimille among others. With increasingly higher boost pressure, power reached 275 HP in 1948 and 350 in 1950.

The year 1949, with no Alfa entries, was used for further development. One-time Alfa Romeo racing boss, Enzo Ferrari, was showing an increasing challenge with his entries, but handling problems continually plagued the Maranello cars.

When Alfa re-emerged in 1950, they were as invincible as ever and won all races (eleven) entered again. But in so doing, they set the measure to which Ferrari had to perform, and his cars steadily improved.

The next year, with the Tipo 159, which was producing 425 HP at 9300 rpm, Alfa narrowly won early season races—the Swiss, Belgian and French GPs—with Ferrari pressing hard to wins in the British, German and Italian events. That set up a very important finale, the Spanish GP.

In that race, Alfa won convincingly to take the marque's fourth season out of five with cars developed from a 13-year-old design. Juan Manuel Fangio took the 1951 Championship, the first of his five titles, in

Alfa Romeo twin-cam Giulia four-cylinder was a well-proven engine when installed in the GTZ. At 122 HP, the cars were highly competitive in the 1.6-liter class.

GTZ interior is functional if not a little stark, but the light weight enabled dazzling performance from such a small engine. Handling and braking were exceptional.

the Tipo 159 Alfetta.

    With that victory, Alfa Romeo retired from racing. It was 1960 before the marque was racing again, sort of through the back door, with a production car aimed at racing by customers rather than factory teams. That was the Giulietta SZ (Sprint Zagato). The SZ was the interim step leading to another racing car based on the Giulia line but really carrying only the Giulia name, the TZ. Its design was very different from the planned Giulia line.

    The GTZ was built on a tubular spaceframe with an aluminum body that was both aerodynamic and aesthetically pleasing in design. Its suspension was all-independent of modern design with four-wheel disc brakes. The purpose: Alfa Romeo was back into racing in a big way with a

factory team and plans were made to offer similar cars to the racing public.

    However, readying the Giulia 1600 for production required the efforts of the TZ team, so the factory chose to establish a new racing department to develop and campaign the cars and their successors. Autodelta, headed by well-experienced ex-Ferrari engineer Carlo Chiti, became Alfa's racing arm.

    By the time Autodelta entered its first proper race, it was 1964 and the cars had gone through five years of development. The result was class wins at Sebring, LeMans, the Targa Florio and at Nurburgring.

    At Sebring, the Stoddard/Kaser Team finished 188 laps with a 13th overall. LeMans saw the Businello/Deserti team also finishing 13th over-

chassis were constructed of honeycomb aluminum and glue, a technique derived from Ford's space programs, rather than sheet-steel tubs like the earlier cars.

Beginning where Ford left off the year before, Mario Andretti and Bruce McLaren won Sebring in a Mk IV by completing 238 laps (1237 miles) in 12 hours. A.J. Foyt and Lloyd Ruby took second with a Mk II finishing 226 laps. Unfortunately, Ken Miles had been killed while testing a prototype J-car.

FORD GT-40
1966

4738cc/289-CID cast-iron OHV V8
390 HP @ 7000 rpm
5-speed ZF transaxle
2440 lb, fiberglass doors, front and rear body sections
steel monocoque chassis with subframes
all independent coil-spring suspension

Four Mk IVs were entered at LeMans '67 and were simply overwhelming until a crash took out two of the cars and renewed hopes in the Ferrari pits that they at least had a chance. But that was not to be. Ferrari was back with 330 P4s with more horsepower and less weight than the earlier P3, 450 HP at 8000 rpm and 1760 pounds. The Mk IV ran 7-liter NASCAR engines again, but this time with dual Holley four-barrel carbs producing 500 HP at 6400 rpm. Weight was also down to just under 2600 pounds, but the P4 still held a decided advantage, 0.26 power-to-weight ratio compared to 0.19 of the Mk IV.

At LeMans, Jim Hall's 7-liter Chaparral 2F coupes were a definite threat to the Mk IV, but failed to go the distance. With Hall out due to mechanical problems, the '67 race was a straight Ford-Ferrari dual. But Gurney and Foyt were unassailable, scoring the first all-American (both drivers and car) victory in the history of the LeMans 24-Hours. Setting two new records for both speed and distance, they averaged 135.48 mph for 3251.57 miles, marks not exceeded until the coming of the 917K Porsches in 1970. Ford won the International Championship for Sports Cars while Ferrari took the International Championship for Sports-Prototypes.

From winning LeMans again, the international rules quickly changed to outlaw the big Fords. Prototypes could run no larger than 3-liter engines although sports cars were allowed up to 5 liters. And the Mk I GT-40s were still around to be a thorn in the side of Ferrari and newcomer to the front ranks, Porsche.

In final development, the Mk I GT-40 was updated by Len Bailey to produce the first Mirage, a sleeker, lighter car. This is the only surviving example and is the winner of four major races as one of the blue and orange John Wyer Gulf-Ford team cars.

John Wyer campaigned the Gulf-Ford GT-40 team of 5-liter sports cars and returned to LeMans in 1968 to humble both Ferrari and Porsche. Pedro Rodriguez and Lucien Bianchi won. In fact, the Gulf-Fords won all but one championship race entered in 1968, and served notice that Ford was still on top of endurance racing. Ford won its fourth World Championship that year.

For 1969, Ferrari's 3-liter prototype 312 P and Porsche's 3-liter prototype 908 came on the scene to unseat the 5-liter GT-40s still running production-based engines producing around 425 HP at 6000 rpm. The 312 P ran 420 HP at 9800 rpm from 2990cc while the 908 developed 350 HP at 8400 rpm from 2977cc. The 312 P was a water-cooled V12; the 908 an air-cooled flat-8. Both were lightweights at around 1500 pounds and both were the cutting edge of new racing technology. The 312 P was a failure, while the 908 emerged supreme.

However the six-year-old GT-40 design driven by Jacky Ickx and Jackie Oliver won both at Sebring and LeMans to give Ford its fourth straight, and last, LeMans victory.

The following year, the blue and orange Gulf colors were applied to Wyer's 917K Porsches that became the big winners.

LOLA T-70

Late version of the T-70, the Mk IIIB-GT of 1969, was Eric Broadley's venture into competition against 3-liter prototypes from Porsche and Ferrari and 5-liter sports cars from both. Porsches proved dominant.

When international racing rules changed for the 1966 season and brought on the Sports-50 class, that automatically made Eric Broadley's Lola T-70 eligible. Not only were open T-70s seen in Can-Am and Interserie racing, they were now going up against cars for the World Sports Car Championship.

Broadley's experience in racing began when his backyard tinkering produced an Austin-7 special, then a Ford Ten special for the 1172 formula of Britain's 750 Motor Club. He and the car immediately began winning races and took the Chapman Cup in 1957 against Lotus 9 and 11 cars with similar Ford Ten engines.

Featherweight Lotus 11s dominated the 1100cc Sports/Racing class, and Eric and his brother Graham undertook a new car to challenge with. It took two years to complete, but when it first raced at Snetterton, the new car in Broadley's hands easily won the 1100 Sport race and equaled the track record.

With a string of wins and more track records, the car received a lot of attention and encouraged civil engineer Broadley to go into car building full time. The result was the founding of Lola Cars Ltd in December, 1958. That began a remarkable climb into world-class racing. Building on

the foundation laid with his first 1100cc car, Broadley built a series of Lolas known as the Mk I.

These cars were powered by Coventry Climax FWA 1098cc engines inclined 10° to the left. Bodies were of aluminum over a tubular space frame, producing an extremely lightweight car of just under 850 pounds. With 90 HP at 7200 rpm and a BMC A-series gearbox having special gear ratios, the Mk I Lola was a formidable opponent.

Win after win and many fastest laps and new records were their forte and brought Lola Cars a lot of attention. That was very encouraging for Broadley, whose small company continually responded with improvements that held sway in its class over Lotus 11s, Elvas, Cooper Tojeiro specials and other one-offs. Not only were Lolas the front runners, they also put it to 1500cc cars on many occasions and usually finished high with an occasional win in that class.

The reason for such success was attributed to Broadley's ability to assimilate the latest ideas and then to top off his creations with his own innovations. In the Mk I, the rear suspension was his own and superb handling was the mark of the cars. Lola Mk Is were one of very few new entries to meet with instant success against tried-and-true competitors.

Their sudden rise was a success story unparalleled in British racing history.

Club racing became Lola Mk I territory, so much so that an example of the Mk I stood alongside the World Sports Car Champion Aston Martin DBR1 at the Racing Car Show in January, 1960. Built into the early 1960s, Lola Mk Is were Broadley's racing cars that laid the base for rapid future growth.

That was provided by Ford who ventured into top-rank racing to challenge Ferrari. Broadley had upped the stakes of his cars by producing his Lola GT. This line of Ford V8 powered mid-engined cars was also intended to face off against the fast Italians in international racing, but only one was sold before Ford selected Broadley and his firm for development of the Ford GT.

From Aston Martin came John Wyer to manage Ford Advanced Vehicles at Slough, England, where the cars were built. Thus, Broadley and Wyer were teamed up on a new venture that pushed Broadley into world-class racing-car design. In association with Wyer and Ford engineers, his job was to produce the chassis and suspension of the new car, and his Lola GT was used as a testbed for development.

When Can-Am racing developed from the Pro-series, one of the top cars was the Lola T-70 shown here in open form. Powered by small-block Chevrolet V8s, these Lolas were formidable opposition.

LOLA T-70 MK IIIB
1969

4990cc/304-CID cast-iron OHV Chevrolet V8
430 HP @ 7500 rpm
5-speed Hewland LG600 transmission
1940 lb, aluminum monocoque construction
fiberglass doors, front and rear sections
all independent coil-spring suspension

This began the Ford GT-40 saga, but Broadley tired of the Ford association and returned to Lola to exploit his new knowledge.

In fully developed form, the GT-40 rivaled anything and Broadley's answer was the Lola T-70. Introduced in 1965, the T-70 was intended as a sports/racer with Ford's 4.7-liter engine, the same powerplant as the GT-40. Then in 1966, a shift to Chevrolet 5.4- and 5.9-liter V8s occurred, and in 1967 a magnificent new coupe was introduced. The Lola T-70 was both lighter and faster than a GT-40, but lack of thorough development continually plagued the cars. In theory, if a seasoned team had taken on the cars, they very likely could have become a serious challenger to Ford's GT-40s.

On another front, the Lola T-70 story parallels the emergence of Bruce McLaren's Can-Am cars and were adversaries in that style of racing. Although Lola won the first season of Can-Am racing, the McLarens proved overwhelming after 1966.

When FIA regulations placed a 5-liter limit on sports cars for 1968, T-70s were immediately obsolete. In a heated exchange, FIA bent their rules slightly and homologated the cars as 5-liter sports cars, taking into account all the open and closed T-70s that had been built. When McLaren attempted the same the following year, FIA emphatically declined!

In smaller Group-7 events in Britain, T-70s were usually favorites. Their ferocious look and sound provided huge appeal, but in long-distance racing the cars were plagued by engine, transmission and suspension failures. Although John Surtees had the hot hand in Can-Am racing in 1966, wins by T-70s afterward were rather thin. Championship races were the same story.

In lesser British events of 1968 where the Mk IIIB coupe ran, Brian Redman won the Guards Trophy at Oulton Part, Denny Hulme won the TT and the Martini Trophy and Frank Gardner won the Guards Trophy at Brands Hatch. Thus, in shorter sprint-style races, T-70 Lolas were tough to beat. At Silverstone, T-70s were 1-2-3 with Hulme, Redman and Paul Hawkins. Hawkins and Jo Bonnier took the Guards Trophy at Snetterton 1-2. Thruxton was another 1-2-3 sweep for Redman, Bonnier and Hawkins. David Piper won at Montlhery in France and other wins followed, showing the T-70 was indeed a formidable machine.

During the years of 1967 and '68, they had the potential to be top-rank cars in international racing, but that changed in 1969. FIA regulations dropped 5-liter sports-car production requirements from 50 to 25 units. With that inducement, both Ferrari and Porsche responded with their 512s and 917s, respectively. T-70s were instantly obsolete, a crushing blow to their potential and to Broadley's small firm.

In typical Mk IIIB form, Chevy V8s of 4 X 3-inch bore and stroke, displacing 4990cc (305 cubic inches), produced 430 HP at 7300 rpm on Webers and a compression ratio of 11:1. Otherwise, the Chevrolet engines were conventional overhead-valve types derived from production-based equipment. A Hewland five-speed LG600 transmission backed up the engine and healthy 12-inch Girling disc brakes all around gave the 1940-pound cars excellent stopping power. Bodies were fiberglass over an aluminum monocoque chassis.

The right combination of aerodynamics, acceleration, handling and stopping are the ingredients in any successful racing car, and the Lola T-70 combined them all in excellent proportion.

PORSCHE CARRERA-6

The 906 won its class in its first race, the 24-Hour Daytona Continental of 1966. Blue was a new color to Porsche and few spectators recognized the significance of the new shape and color, a revolution in sports-car design from Porsche.

First of a new generation of Porsches, the Type 906 (also known as the Carrera-6) was a 2-liter champion in a class by itself. Aerodynamically efficient as only the scientific approach to design allows, the 906 launched Porsche toward world domination of sports-car racing.

The Porsche Carrera-6, known internally as the Type 906, was the result of a new approach undertaken by the newly formed Racing Vehicle Design department at Zuffenhausen. Thoroughly scientific in its approach, rather than the conventional "if it looks right, it is right" method, the new team launched Porsche toward greatness.

In charge was Ferdinand Piech, just 26 years old, the grandson of the elder Dr. Porsche and son of Dr. Ferry Porsche's sister. His job was to lead the design and development of the Type 906, supervise racing, prepare the teams and determine the entries of drivers and cars.

That was a vast undertaking, but the 906 proved so good, it convincingly showed that Piech and his youthful team had the right stuff.

The origin of the 906 came about as has many other racing cars, from the challenge presented by competitors. In this case, Ferrari. Porsche had long dominated the European Hill Climb Championship,

The torsional stiffness of the 906 tubular space frame was 1400 lb-ft per degree, about the same as the 904/6 coupe chassis but achieved with substantially less weight. In order to meet homologation requirements in time to be approved by FIA; Porsche contracted out the manufacture of 50 frames to Karosseriewerk Weinsberg under the direction of Ing. Wilhelm Hild, a strong advocate of Porsche racing.

Bodies for the 906 were also contracted out to save time. These fiberglass-reinforced polyester structures were not used for chassis strengthening, unlike the 904, so they were made both thinner and lighter. The number of panels required of the 904, about 50, was reduced by about half in the 906. Its frontal area was 14.26 square feet, about the same as the 904, although nearly 6 inches wider, and gave an aerodynamic drag coefficient of 0.35, slightly higher than the 904. A low, downsloped front section was designed to reduce front-end lift, one of the faults of the 904 at high speed. A rear spoiler was incorporated into the final body configuration and whisker spoilers were added to works cars when wind-tunnel tests showed they further reduced front-end lift. Overall height was just 38.6 inches.

PORSCHE 906
1966

1991cc/121-CID SOHC air-cooled alloy flat 6-cylinder
220 HP @ 8000 rpm
5-speed Porsche transaxle
1341 lb, fiberglass body w/tubular spaceframe chassis
all independent coil-spring suspension

The cockpit shape was accentuated by rounded side windows and windshield that melded into a sloping aft section fitted with a large louvered clear-plastic cover. With the high fenders, rounded cockpit and gullwing doors, the radical shape of the 906 was a favorite among photographers and was dubbed the "Batmobile."

Inside was pure function, only a few switches; a tach and a combination oil-temperature/oil-pressure gage monitored the engine. The driver sat in a low, reclining position.

The power train of the 904/6 was well-proven, and when fitted to the new 906, a seasoned racing car was born. The engine was a modified version of the 911 production-car engine introduced in 1964, rather than an exotic racing design. This six-cylinder was designated the Type 901/20 with carburetors, and later the Type 901/21 when improved with Bosch fuel injection.

By using magnesium in place of aluminum and titanium instead of steel, engine weight dropped dramatically from 405 pounds to just 296, even less than the four-cylinder that powered the 904.

The compression ratio of the Type 901 engine was 10.3:1 and each combustion chamber was fired by dual plugs from a four-breaker Marelli distributor. Valve ports were enlarged from 32mm to about 40mm and sodium-filled valves were used. The Type 901/20 engines received triple-throat 46mm Webers, type 46IDA3C, and each bank of cylinders ex-

FIA regulations required a two-place configuration, and two people could conceivably travel in reasonable comfort in a 906. But later cars of still greater efficiency turned passenger accommodations into a joke as FIA relaxed its sports-car requirements in favor of prototypes.

but Scarfiotti came on strong in late 1965 with the lower, lighter Ferrari Dino to end the success of the special lightweight factory eight-cylinder Spyders.

Porsche quickly responded with a spectacularly successful hillclimb car that laid the conceptual foundation for the Carrera 6. Porsche had employed tubular space frames in earlier Spyders and revived it in that car and the Type 906.

For 1966, Porsche planned to produce a Grand Touring coupe based on the 904 and using a modified 911 engine to race in FIA's new Sports Car Class where 50 or more cars had to be built. Following hillclimb successes, design concepts centered on a radically different approach rather than reworking the 904, itself a successful car but at the end of its competitive lifetime.

The 906 had a wheelbase of 90.6 inches, the same as the 904, but with track widths of 52.7 inches in the front (about an inch wider than the 904) and a rear track of 55.2 inches (3.3 inches wider than the 904). Overall width came out at 66.1 inches because of wider wheels and tires, a full 5.5-inches wider than the 904. Two quarter-cylindrical fuel tanks were fitted under the door sills, one on either side, and held 26.4 gallons (100 liters) total.

The Type 906, Porsche's mid-engine Grand Touring coupe of 1966, was powered by a modified 911 six-cylinder engine, the Type 901/20 with 46IDA3C triple-throat Webers. Weighing a mere 286 lb, engine output was 220 HP at 8200 rpm with a top speed over 167 mph.

hausted into its own tube header and slightly flared megaphone tip. Factory racing engines gave about 225 HP at 8200 rpm. Torque peaked at 145 lb-ft at 6000 rpm.

Substantial weight reduction throughout the car gave a final race weight of 1366 pounds dry, a full 174 less than the 904. With the five-speed transaxle came a huge variety of gearing—33 gearsets spanning every conceivable need. First road-holding tests returned a lateral acceleration of 1.125 g, a significant advance on the best achieved by the 904 at 1.1 g. Offered at $11,500, 50 Carrera 6 racing cars had no difficulty being placed in the hands of serious Porsche racing teams.

The first 906 to appear in competition was at the Daytona Continental 24-Hour of January, 1966. It was the first 906 built and was driven to a resounding first-time-out class victory and sixth overall by Hans Herrmann and Gerhard Mitter. By the February running of the Sebring 12-Hour, five cars had been completed and on the starting line: two works cars and three private entries. This was the first showdown between the 906 and Ferrari's Dino, a single car driven by Lorenzo Bandini and Ludovico Scarfiotti. Through the fifth hour, the Dino lead the 906s, but at the finish it was a works 906 ahead of the Dino for another class victory, the second in succession for the 906.

Drivers in the class winner were Herrmann, Mitten and long-time Porsche racer, American driver Joe Buzzetta. The fourth-place 906 remained in the United States for Buzzetta to campaign in the under-2-liter class in the USRRC (United States Road Racing Championship). Other drivers of 906s in the USRRC were Ken Miles, Don Wester and Scooter Patrick. These cars and drivers dominated the series with Patrick taking Otto Zipper's Russkit-sponsored 906 to victory. Buzzetta finished second in the tough series, giving Porsche a clean sweep.

First racing in prototype class, the 906 was homologated as a Group 4 Sports Car on May 1st, 1966, after 50 had been built. Two works cars were entered in the Monza 1000 Km of April, 1966, along with three additional private entries. On Ferrari's home turf, it was a classic battle in the Dino/Carrera 6 war with the 906s taking the victory, a second, third, fourth and sixth in prototype with Dinos fifth and seventh.

Dinos never qualified as Group 4 Sports Cars due to insufficient numbers, and always raced in prototype. But by the May 8th running of Italy's famed Targa Florio, the 906 had been designated a Group 4 car. Another face-off for these small-engine cars, Porsche again trounced the works Ferraris by winning the event overall, a resounding victory for the 906, Porsche's mainline racing car.

Siffert and Davis finished fourth overall behind the winning trio of Fords at LeMans, 1966, and won the 2-liter class and the Index of Performance by finishing 2834.77 miles at 118.12 mph. For a six-cylinder, under-2-liter car, that was a momentous finish. It was just one of many victories taken by the 906, the first of the new generation Porsches that soon became the dominant force in international racing.

SUNBEAM TIGER

At speed in British racing green, the Sunbeam Tiger of 1964 first came with a 260-CID Ford V8, then later with a 289. A tough Ford *top-loader* four-speed transmissions matched to Salisbury rear-axle assembly made a strong performance combination, "the fastest car in the world for under $3500" as advertised.

The origin of the Sunbeam Tiger was inspired by the success of Carroll Shelby's Cobra. Shelby transformed the AC Ace into the Cobra by fitting Ford's new-technology Fairlane V8 engine in place of the more-traditional British six-banger. Using that idea, Ian Garrad approached the anemic Sunbeam Alpine with the same V8.

Garrad was west-coast USA manager for the Rootes Group, builder of the cars through their Sunbeam-Talbot division in Coventry, England. Sunbeam had once been Britain's premier racing marque, and according to Ian's father, Norman Garrad—Rootes Group competition manager for about twenty years—the Alpine introduced in 1957 became one of the most successful production sports cars of all time. They took some 165 awards in all sorts of international competition and won the prestigious Index of Thermal Efficiency at LeMans in 1961.

The Index ranked second to overall victory, the two most sought after achievements at LeMans, and was awarded to the car showing the highest performance for its weight on the least amount of fuel.

Ian Garrad had learned the fortunes of Sunbeam racing first hand from his father's involvement at Rootes. He knew that Sunbeam drivers Stirling Moss, Jack Brabham, Mike Hawthorn, Graham Hill, John Fitch and others had been successful in Sunbeams, but they had also recommended more power so the cars could be even more competitive. In response, the factory investigated the possibility of Ferrari manufacturing a high-performance crossflow head with Weber carburetors for their four-cylinder engine. But that project didn't materialize.

SUNBEAM TIGER
1966

4262cc/260-CID cast-iron OHV Ford V8
245 HP @ 5400 rpm
Ford 4-speed transmission
2565 lb, steel unit-body/frame
independent coil-spring front suspension
leaf-spring live-axle rear suspension

In southern California, Ian Garrad learned the sunshine state's solution for low performance—engine swaps. Secretly, he siphoned-off advertising funds to build two V8 Alpine prototypes. Successful Alpine racer Ken Miles and Garrad did a quick weekend engine swap to test the idea and find out if Ford's lightweight, thinwall V8 would fit into the Alpine's small engine compartment. The cost was only $600, a small sum to start a legend.

Miles and Garrad fitted the engine and an automatic transmission to an Alpine, and after torrid midnight rides in heavy rains with a terrified Garrad aboard, Miles proclaimed the Alpine V8 to have fantastic potential. With that success, Garrad tabbed Shelby to do a thoroughly

Probably one of the tightest fits the small-block Ford V8 ever encountered, the Sunbeam Tiger's unibody construction provided some engineering challenges to accept the engine. But the resulting package packed a lot of punch.

engineered prototype. Shelby American employee George Boskoff handled the project and produced a well thought out prototype. That cost $10,000 and launched the Tiger for real. The time was April, 1963.

Fully tested in all sorts of conditions and weather, the Shelby prototype met the rigors of American driving from the mountains to the sea and paved the way for Sunbeam's most awesome modern sports car. Unknown to the factory, Garrad had undertaken the Americanization of the Alpine and was rewarded with a cool reception when the car was introduced at Coventry.

Factory management virtually ignored Garrad's Alpine, dubbed the "Thunderbolt," until it was test driven. The car was an exciting performer unlike anything they had ever built. It quickly went up the line to Lord Rootes himself who drove the car and proclaimed it to be Sunbeam's new "Tiger." The name was in honor of Sir Henry Segrave's Sunbeam-powered land-speed record car of 1926, named the Tiger. (Segrave set the world land-speed record of 152.33 mph, a whopping speed for the time.)

Sunbeam engineering went through the Shelby prototype to refine it for production. A Salisbury rear-end assembly with gears of the Cobra and Jaguar sort were added along with stronger springs. In April, 1964, the Sunbeam Tiger was first shown to the public at the 8th annual International Auto Show in New York. At the time, there was some confusion over the name: Thunderbolt, Tiger or its European designation of Alpine 260 (for its Ford 260-CID engine). But "Tiger" was its name

and "Hold that Tiger" became the sales jargon at shows. Carroll Shelby was shown in early advertisements saying, "You don't turn it on, you unleash it!"

The new line of cars was registered with FIA and SCCA for racing. Sunbeam showrooms had a new entrant in the high-performance sports-car field and road racers had a hot new production roadster. The factory developed heavy-duty suspension packages for all sorts of competition from rallies to ice racing, including endurance racing at LeMans where three special coupes were built for Rootes by Brian Lister for that 24-hour enduro. These LeMans Tigers produced respectable times for steel-bodied cars and turned in average lap speeds around the 8.3-mile Sarthe circuit of 113 mph, compared to the winning Ferrari prototype race average of 121.56 mph.

For the American market, Garrad and Shelby developed an extensive line of options, designated the LAT options, that covered everything from performance parts to racing jackets. Through dealers, buyers could order their Tigers from the stock two-barrel version at 164 HP to a superb handling Stage III, 245-HP tire burner. Alpines in racing tune produced about 115 HP, so the V8 in its most basic form was a sizable step up in performance. The 245-HP, four-barrel versions were positively electrifying.

Performance depended on equipment and final-drive gearing. Rear-end ratios ranged from 2.88:1, giving Tigers top speeds over 155 mph, to optional 4.55:1 gears that produced drag-racing stats of 108 mph at 12.95 seconds in the 1/4-mile. Those figures were produced by a Tiger that held AHRA class world records in both speed and elapsed time for at least two years.

In international racing, Tigers were excellent rally cars taking 1-2-3 in the over-2500cc GT class of the 1964 Geneva Rally. In 1965, the cars took a 1-2 in the same class of the Monte Carlo Rally, a first in the International Police Rally, a first in the Scottish International Rally and were first in the Dutch National 24-Hour, setting a new speed record.

One of the Lister Tigers was campaigned privately in the 1965 European Autosport Championship. Having won over such cars as Lightweight E-type Jaguars and Cobras, the Tiger was in contention for the close-fought championship until the last race. While leading, its hood popped up resulting in a DNF.

In European races, Tigers were known as Sunbeam 260, and their entries were few because most Europeans were not familiar with the Ford V8 engine. Thus, they were not very popular although the Tuerlinx/Roets team won the GT over-2-liter class, finishing 13th overall in the 1000 Km of Spa-Francorchamps in 1967.

Originally in the B/Production class of SCCA sports-car racing in America, and later C/Production, Tigers won the PaCoast B/P Divisional, the USRRC "Badger 200" at Road America and the US 200 National Sports car race. The following year, 1965, Tigers took two first overall wins, six 1st-in-class wins and finished the American Road Race of Champions (ARRC) for the National Championship in second place overall ahead of a Shelby GT-350R Mustang.

Thus, for their brief existence, 1964 through 1967, Tigers proved to have excellent potential in racing. All totaled, 7083 Tigers were built in three series with 5109 imported to the US.

it. Shelby's team of Cobras, GT-350 Mustangs and GT-40s backed up by independents bowled over the competition for a period of five years; there was little left for other marques.

The 427 Cobra was the logical extension of the 289 Cobra and came in response to Ferrari's threat of building a new GT car to retain the World Manufacturer's Championship nearly lost to Shelby's team of 289 Cobras in 1964. Ferrari failed to make FIA homologation of his cars, so Maranello withdrew its 250 GTO cars from factory GT racing and Shelby's Daytona Coupes and FIA roadsters took the title in 1965.

Thus, the need for the 427 Cobra passed without confrontation on the international level. On the American scene, two early full-spec competition 427 roadsters were consistent enough to receive invitations to the year-end runoffs for the National Championships. Independents Hal Keck and George Montgomery finished 1-2 for an A/Production clean sweep. The 427 Cobras went on to win that title in 1966, '67, '68 and '73—six years after production of 427 Cobras ended in 1967.

The first prototype 427 was little more than a 289 Cobra with a NASCAR 427 engine shoehorned in. Works driver Ken Miles raced it at Sebring, 1964, to test the idea. He led a Corvette Grand Sport until sidelined by mechanical problems. With the likes of Chevrolet racing the blisteringly fast Grand Sport 'Vettes, Shelby had a new reason for the 427.

Beginning with a modern coil-spring chassis based on a good deal of GT-40 theory, the 427 Cobra frame was built on 3.5-inch-OD twin steel tubes in a ladder configuration and positioned 2.5-inches wider than the 289 Cobra frame. This chassis and suspension design was far superior to the earlier leaf-spring cars. Chassis and aluminum bodies continued to be built by AC Cars, Ltd., and were shipped to Shelby American in Los Angeles for completion. They were about 7 inches wider than the 289 Cobra, about 400 pounds heavier at 2400 pounds and got about 150 more horsepower.

In stock form, Ford's highly proven NASCAR side-oiler 427-CID engine was listed to produce 425 HP with one four-barrel Holley carburetor. But that was underestimated; they actually produced around 500!

Only about a dozen full-spec racing-model 427 Cobras were built. List price was $9800. Following them were the very similar S/C model at about $7800. Because there was no factory 427 Cobra racing team, the five SCCA A/P National Championships won by the 4-bbl 427-CID Cobras were taken by private teams.

Except for hood, doors, interior and windshield, the 427 Cobras were very different roadsters than the 289s. Everything the 289s did, the 427s did better, except for international racing where the 289s were the big winners.

At $7495, a street 427 Cobra wasn't cheap. Full-spec competition roadsters cost about $9800 and gave 175 mph in open-roadster form. Factory-built Dragonsnakes listed for $10,485, the fastest production bullet ever produced in sports-car guise.

157

FERRARI 330 P3

This 1967 Ferrari P3/4 shows the striking styling of Maranello's prototype V12. This was a factory design with fabrication by Drogo which must remain as one of the all-time great racing-car designs.

Maranello continued development of prototype cars for championship racing and introduced the strikingly handsome 330 P3 at Sebring in 1966. The smooth, flowing coachwork of curving aluminum panels no doubt remains among the most sensuous of all Ferraris.

The origin of the P3 rose from the 330 P2 introduced in April, 1965. John Surtees and Ludovico Scarfiotti gave the P2 its biggest victory at Nurburgring in the 1000 Km, much to the dismay of Porsche fans. In return, Porsche was showing superb form in Sicily's Targa Florio by winning the 1963 and 1964 rounds. Fans wanted Ferrari to win and organizers responded by creating a new class, called the Italian GT, to entice Maranello to return in full force.

Enzo responded by sending three of his 275 P ("P" for prototype) cars to the 1965 event to regain the Italian pride. The 275 P, and its close cousin the 250 LM, were in top form that year as demonstrated by Bandini and Vaccarella winning the Targa with an average of 63.59 mph over the 446.4 tortuous miles of the Sicilian circuit. Bending the rules had worked and gave Targa fans what they wanted.

The 275 P was in top form, and by 1966 it had reached the 50-unit mark for homologation as a Group 4 sports car, the 250 LM, to contest Ford's GT-40s. In the Prototype class, Ferrari continued on with the V12 line in the 330 P of 1964 to take full advantage of the 4-liter prototype rules. Its 60° V12 engine was essentially two 2-liter V6 Dinos back-to-back, giving 3967cc.

In original form, the 330 P of 1964 was a two-cammer (single overhead cam on each bank) with six dual-choke 38 DCN Webers delivering 370 HP from a 9.8:1 compression ratio on gasoline. Fitted into the

The P3/4 V12 is DOHC 60° design by Rocchi with a bore and stroke of 77 X 71mm giving 3967cc displacement. Compression ratio of 11.1:1 yielded 450 HP at 8000 rpm with Lucas fuel injection.

Although the 275 P forebears of the 330 P3/4 had shown brilliantly in international racing, stiff competition in the form of stock-block 7-liter prototype Fords made racing tough. Ford won at LeMans, but Ferrari won the Manufacturer's Championship of 1967 with 34 points to Porsche's 32 and Ford's 22.

back of the 275 P, it instantly gave a 50-HP increase over the earlier 3 liter. In another car of wider stance and revised suspension to put more power to the ground, the 330 P2 was born.

At the same time, a new head layout produced another engine of greater complexity. This was a double-overhead-cam design with revised combustion chambers and improved breathing that produced 410 HP at its peak, 8200 rpm, using larger 40 DCN/2 Webers. With higher compression ratio, 10.5:1, and using Lucas fuel injection, this engine became the 330 P3, delivering 420 HP at 8200 rpm.

The P3 was the big gun in Ferrari's anti-Ford campaign in 1966 and an impressive racing machine. However, the season began badly as Ford won both Daytona and Sebring. To get back into the swing of things, Ferrari had to win a big one. Under such pressure, the Surtees/Parkes team won at Monza, the 1000 Km, in their P3 with two GT-40s trailing second and third. Thus, Maranello was well behind in championship points, but the P3 was quite capable of besting the Fords if they proved as reliable as the GT-40s.

Attempting to secure another win in the Targa Florio, works Ferraris found racing in the wet to be tough going, and the factory Porsches were in top form. At the end, Porsche took another of its many Targa

wins with Ferrari having to settle for second.

Mike Parkes and Scarfiotti showed the truest form of the P3 in the fast Spa-Francorchamps 1000 Km where they won convincingly with a 131.69-mph race average and set an absolute lap record of 139 mph. But even though the Spa tuneup for LeMans looked very good for Ferrari, Nurburgring was to see another contender chip away at Maranello's chances.

Jim Hall's Chaparral-2D was in top form in the hands of Phil Hill and Jo Bonnier who won at 89.3-mph average, the marque's only endurance win in 1966. Surtees and Scarfiotti had won the 'Ring the year before in a 330 P2, but the P3 was denied.

LeMans '66 showed Ford with the largest contingent, eight 7-liter Mk IIs in prototype class backed by five 4.7-liter GT-40 sports cars. Ferrari had fielded 10 cars in 1965 and earned a win that year, but eleven cars in 1966, including three P3s, was to prove disastrous.

Labor disputes had broken out at Maranello and the cars did not receive proper preparation. The P3s hadn't been touched since the previous race. At LeMans, Surtees quarreled with team-manager Dragoni over Scarfiotti being listed as the third driver with him and Parkes and walked out claiming preferential treatment toward Italian drivers.

Three Ferrari Dinos and a P2 converted to P3 specifications broke in the third hour and were out. Scarfiotti crashed his P3 while holding second place, and Luigi Chinetti's NART P2 went out with transmission problems. All the other big Ferraris went out with a variety of ills and only two Ferraris, both 275 GTBs, were still running at the finish. Le-Mans was a Ford 1-2-3 sweep. The GT-40s just didn't break.

FERRARI 330 P3/4
1967

3967cc/242-CID DOHC 36-valve V12
450 HP @ 8000 rpm
Ferrari 5-speed transaxle
1890 lb, fiberglass/aluminum body w/aluminum tubular frame
all independent coil-spring suspension

With no hope of another championship, the P3s did little during the remainder of the season and some were sold to privateers.

In December of 1966, a revised version was tested at Daytona. This was the 330 P4. Although retaining the same basic engine, power was brought up to 450 HP at 8000 rpm with a 36-valve, DOHC arrangement, two intakes and one exhaust per cylinder. Two sparkplugs and four coils were used, derived from the Formula 1 powerplant Ferrari raced at Monza. A new Ferrari-designed and built transaxle replaced the ZF unit.

The 1967 season was obviously to be a clash of the titans, Ferrari against Ford again with both Chaparral and Porsche being strong contenders. At Daytona, the P4 looked very good with Chris Amon and Lorenzo Bandini leading a spectacular P4 1-2-3 sweep, letting Ford know that Ferrari was back. Ford was also back with a lighter, faster, more-powerful replacement for the GT-40, known as the Mk IV, still running

production-based 7-liter engines. Mario Andretti and Bruce McLaren responded to the Ferrari threat by winning Sebring with 238 laps, ten more than the Ken Miles/Lloyd Ruby Mk II winner in 1966.

The Bandini/Amon P4 came back by leading a 1-2 P4 victory at Monza with a P3 in fourth. Ferrari proved to be on even terms with Ford. But then a variant of the GT-40, John Wyer's Mirage, won at Spa, and Porsche moved into the spoiler's slot at the Targa Florio by taking another win in spite of a P4—a P3 upped to P4 specs—and a 330 LM, which all failed to place.

Nurburgring was overwhelmed by Porsche, a 1-2-3-4 rout of everything else, and LeMans was seen to be an intense but classic dual. Fifty-four starters included four Mk IV and three Mk II 7-liter Fords, backed by three 4.7-liter GT-40s. Seven P4s led Ferrari's assault of the prototype class, although some were updated P3s, and showed that the Italians were serious about regaining their pride on the famed Sarthe circuit of 8.3 miles.

The LeMans 24-Hours involved almost 7000 gear changes during some 390 laps of 35 to more than 200 mph. The P4s were lighter, quicker and better handlers than the Fords, but durability was also a key part of endurance racing, and the Mk IVs were extremely durable. With the Dan Gurney/A.J. Foyt Mk IV leading from the second hour, the Ferraris found closing the gap in the final hours impossible. Although the P4s were lapping 10 seconds a lap faster, the Americans made no mistakes and led to the end with two P4s following. Scarfiotti and Parkes averaged 134.13 mph for 3219.13 miles behind the winning Ford that averaged just 1.36 mph faster, going 32.5 miles further during the 24-Hours. Those stats would have established both speed and distance records for Ferrari had the P4 won.

Ford proved itself at LeMans again, but Ferrari won the World Championship for Sports/Prototypes over 2 liters. Even though LeMans was lost, it was clear that Ferrari was back in the form of earlier years with the 330 P3 and P4 prototypes.

Third-series Type 908 Porsches were known as "Flounders" due to their flat shape. Jo Siffert and Brian Redman, Porsche's leading driver team in 1969, won Brands Hatch, Nurburgring and Watkins Glen in Flounders and won both the Monza and Spa 1000 Km races in long-tail coupes to clinch the World Championship of Makes.

The fuel-injected Type 908 eight-cylinder as fitted to 908/2 Flounders. Basically a rather simple engine in concept, the Type 908 proved to be highly reliable and durable.

coupes, they won the Monza 1000 Km and the Spa 1000 Km where they led a grand Porsche finish of 1-2-3-4-5 overall. Redman set a new lap record at Spa, 3 minutes 37 seconds in 908/01-025, the Lang Heck coupe shown here. In his hands, it gave 199-mph top speed.

The 908s finished several races in sweeps and won the World Championship before the running of LeMans, 1969. Confident of victory with seasoned cars and teams, the Porsches rolled out at the start only to have new 917s lead for more than 21 hours. That was both unexpected and exciting, but they were unable to last to the finish. Characteristic of endurance racing where the fastest cars have a habit of not finishing, even the 908s met with failures. Only one was left toward the end and formed the duo of cars that produced the closest fought fender-to-fender dash to the checkered flag in LeMans history.

Porsche nemesis, Wyer's GT-40 Ford driven by the youthful and sensational Jacky Ickx, faced off against veteran Hans Herrmann. Their race involved rising from back markers to the lead when the faster Porsches dropped out. The durability of the GT-40 showed to be its greatest asset while the handling of the 908 was the Porsche's long suit.

After a lengthy pit stop early on to repair the front suspension, Herrmann and Larrousse ran their 908 to its limits to get back into the race. By the time they caught the GT-40, the car's brakes were about gone and required careful driving.

From there on, Herrmann and Ickx produced the most-exciting finish in modern LeMans history, an unmatched classic of classics. After 24 hours and over 3100 miles of racing, the cars finished in a near dead heat. Having dominated the event from the beginning, it was a great disappointment when Herrmann finished an official 396 feet behind Ickx driving the same car that won the 24-Hours the year before. The GT-40 also won the Index of Thermal Efficiency with the 908 taking the 3-liter Sport-Prototype class.

That was the last big win for Ford, but Porsche was just beginning. The 908 in its three forms was the vanguard of endurance racing, a technical masterpiece that set world-class racing on a new course. Ferrari's 312P and its varieties were Italy's challengers, but to no avail. Porsche had become king of the racing world.

FERRARI 312 & 512

The 312 PB (Prototipo Boxer) was developed during the 1971 season and proved to be a strong contender in the 1972 FIA season for 3-liter cars. The 312 PB 12-cylinder Ferrari displaced 2991cc from a bore and stroke of 80 X 46.9mm. Lucas fuel injection and a compression ratio of 11.5:1 produced 450 HP at 10,800 rpm. Top speed was 200 mph.

International rules held both 3-liter Prototype and 5-liter Sports Car categories open to manufacturers in 1968 following FIA's ruling against 7-liter prototypes in 1967. Although that ruling got rid of Ford's 7-liter LeMans-winning Mk IVs, it also caught Ferrari in the midst of upgrading his P4s to be even more competitive.

The P4s had won FIA's Championship of Makes in 1967 and showed themselves to be another supreme Ferrari. But with his biggest gun now obsolete because of the hastily imposed rules, Enzo protested by declaring that there would be no prototype Ferraris from the factory in 1968, and there were none.

Meanwhile, Porsche was developing both the 3-liter 908s for Prototype racing in 1969 and the 4.5-liter 917s to contest the Sports Car category. Thus, Zuffenhausen was going after international racing with vigor.

Having to rethink his commitment, Ferrari put together a team to develop a 3-liter prototype. Toward the end of the 1968 season, the car was nearing completion. Thus, the origin of the 312 P.

Although considerably less formidable than the earlier P4s, the 312 P opened a new chapter in Ferrari full-body racing as shown later in the 312 PBs. But the 312 P story was not a happy one. Against the 908 and 917 Porsches, these Ferraris found the going tough and had little success. Their achievements were two seconds and a fourth in the 1969 season against overwhelming wins by Porsche's 3-liter 908s.

winning the Prototype class and the Index of Performance. (A 914/6 won the 2-liter class, finishing sixth overall and a 911S won the 2.5-liter class at seventh for a clean sweep that year for Porsche.)

Porsche won seven of 10 championship races in 1969, mostly with the 908s, while 917s took one, the Austrian 1000 Km. In 1970, Porsche won nine of 10 championship races, with the 917K winning all but two. The 908s won those, and frequent second- and third-place finishes showed that Porsche built the best racing cars in the world, and had emerged from small-engine classes to dominate worldwide racing. For 1971, Porsche took eight of 11 championship races, with the 917K winning all but the Nurburgring 1000 Km that was won by 908s in the top three positions. With such success, it would be easier to list the races Porsche did not win.

PORSCHE 917K
1970

4907cc/299-CID DOHC air-cooled alloy flat 12
600 HP @ 8400 rpm
5-speed transaxle
1819 lb, fiberglass body w/tubular aluminum space frame
all independent coil-spring suspension

Porsche built the 917 to compete in the international sports-car class where a minimum of 25 were required for homologation. Of that number, some were customer cars like this example that was once licensed for street use in Germany!

The 917K succeeded in fulfilling half of Porsche's longterm goals, winning at LeMans. Their second win there was in '71 where 917Ks finished 1—2 with the Marko/van Lennep car really upping the stakes by setting new speed and distance records, 138.13 mph for 3315.20 miles. The second-place car also beat all previous records and both ran 4907cc engines.

Porsche's superb flat 12-cylinder Type 917 air-cooled engine began with 4.5-liters and later went to 4.9-liters, developing 520 to 580 HP at 8500 rpm. When Ferrari introduced its 512 M (a 5-liter car) at the end of the 1970 season, Porsche upped its 917 to 4998cc, just two under the 5-liter limit set by FIA Group 5 Sports Car rules. This engine first developed 600 HP then went to 630 HP at 8000 rpm when new reduced-friction coating material (nickel silicon carbide) was applied to cylinder bores. To counter expected threats from Ferrari, Porsche developed a 16-cylinder engine that produced 690 HP, but was never actually raced as it was not needed; the Type 917 was unbeatable.

The 12-cylinder 917K engine pushed early short-tail coupes to 218

mph and later Gulf-Porsche long-tail coupes to an incredible timed speed of 241 mph down the long Mulsanne Straight at LeMans. In 1971, Jackie Oliver posted the fastest average lap ever at 151.85 mph in a Gulf-Porsche 917LH, by then developed into a very stable long-tail coupe. The 917K Porsches regularly did over 200 mph, not only at LeMans but also at Monza and Spa.

Because of Porsche's total domination of international endurance racing, FIA rule changes banned the 917s after the 1971 season by limiting engine size to 3-liters and imposed minimum weight limits as well. That combination hit both advantages of the 917, and if Porsche were to race 917s at all, it had to be Can-Am style which they did beginning in 1972.

Not counting frame serial numbers used to rebuild wrecks, a total of 40 Type 917 Porsches were built: 32 short tails, six long tails and two spyders that were the first Can-Am effort from Porsche. The Can-Am shortly became another arena for Zuffenhausen to master.

MUSTANG BOSS 302 TRANS-AM

Bud Moore Trans-Am Mustangs of 1970 were the only Ford factory team that year and regained the crown by soundly beating arch-rival Z-28 Camaro by a sizable margin.

SCCA began the Trans-American Sedan Championship in 1966 as a showcase for production-based cars with an engine-capacity limit of 5-liters. Classes were divided into over- and under-2.5-liter engines. The series grew rapidly, and manufacturers got interested when the Trans-Am's high-caliber racing began drawing hordes of spectators who were sure to identify with "showroom" cars.

To promote manufacturers' interest, SCCA offered a trophy at season's end to the winning marque. Ford wanted to win in any top-drawer racing and went after the Trans-Am with its Mustangs.

Shelby GT-350s were not allowed because they had no rear seat. Without it, they were not sedans. Notchback coupe Mustangs were brought into service and won the Trans-Am in both 1966 and 1967. The 1967 season was with Ford's full factory support of Shelby's Terlingua Racing Team with Jerry Titus driving.

Mustang, the brain-child of Ford vice president Lee Iaccoca, was a smash market success and caught arch-rival Chevrolet napping. GM's response to the sporty Mustang was its equally sporty Camaro first offered in 1967. Although Mercury, Dodge and Plymouth fielded entries in Trans-Am racing, it was the rivalry between Mustang and Camaro that made the series a huge success. Both Ford and GM wanted to win regularly in front of crowds, and mottos ran something like, "win on Sunday, sell on Monday."

Camaro convincingly won the 1968 Trans-Am, and that brought the Boss 302 response from Ford. Ford's failure in 1968 was due mostly to the "tunnel-port" heads run on a new and exceptionally durable four-bolt-main-bearing cast-iron block. To solve the head problem, new canted-valve 351 *Cleveland* heads were installed on the four-bolt-main block to create the Boss 302.

With huge valves, the high-revving Boss 302 engine produced another Ford thoroughbred when the Mustang's first major body redesign came out in 1969. Ford's racing organization, Kar Kraft, built about a

Big-valve 351 Cleveland heads on the four-bolt main-bearing T/A 302 block of 1968 produced a high-winding screamer that turned out 460 HP at 7500 rpm in Trans-Am form with a single Holley four-barrel mated to a Bud Moore Mini-Plenum aluminum intake manifold. The cars were thoroughly developed by Ford's racing arm, Kar Kraft, and sent to Bud Moore Engineering for final preparation.

Stripped to the barest, a heat-protection blanket covered the floorboards of the basic production Mustang. The dash was stock but narrowed in the center to allow rollcage members to be installed along the windshield pillars.

dozen Mustangs for the Trans-Am series during 1969 and '70.

Bud Moore Engineering of Spartanburg, South Carolina, and Shelby-American in California ran Boss 302 teams, but the blue Sunoco-sponsored Z-28 Camaros driven by Mark Donohue won the '69 Trans-Am championship. For 1970, only Moore ran a Trans-Am Mustang team with team drivers Parnelli Jones and George Follmer.

Jones was the lead driver in the three-car team of vibrant-orange Boss 302 Mustangs. They easily won the 1970 Trans-Am title with a point total nearly double that of Camaro. Jones once remarked, "If you're under control, you're not going fast enough!" and that's just the way he drove, even to the extent of leaving Follmer in the dust when there were no other challengers.

The final tally in the T/A championship for '70 was Ford, 72 points, American Motors Javelins, 59 points, with GM's Camaros earning only 40 points in the 11-race schedule. The Bud Moore team took six wins, five seconds and four thirds with Jones taking five of those wins.

The year 1970 was the first to carry Ford's new corporate slogan, "The Sizzlin '70s," that was supposed to carry on the image of the 1960s, "Total Performance." But when corporate racing interests dropped to an all-time low with Ford's withdrawal from factory-sponsored racing in October, 1970, the Trans-Am cars of that year were left as the high-water mark of Ford's interests to race and win on America's road-racing tracks in the 1960s tradition.

MUSTANG T/A BOSS 302
1970

4942cc/302-CID cast-iron OHV V8
460 HP @ 7500 rpm
4-speed transmission
3240 lb, steel unit-body/frame
independent coil-spring front suspension
leaf-spring live-axle rear suspension

The cars carried special serial numbers of 70TA-01 (Follmer's car), 70TA-02 (Jones' lead car) and 70TA-03 as Jones' backup car. They began life as 1969 model fastback Mustangs with Ford's serial numbers of 9F02M212775, 776 and 777. Number 775 was Jones' lead car, 777 his backup and 776 was Follmer's. Even though Jones always ran with number 15 on his car and Follmer with number 16, there was no doubt some mixing of cars and drivers during the season.

Received from Ford in stripped-down condition, the cars went through extensive modification by Kar Kraft. The chassis and body sheet metal were beefed up everywhere with all sorts of trick parts to make the cars as fast, strong, durable and reliable as possible. Tough full-floater rear ends and ultra-strong four-speed transmissions with oil coolers were fitted. These were designed for 200+ mph laps at LeMans without a failure. One testimony to the meaning of "bulletproof" in Ford's Trans-Am racing parts was the fact that the cars didn't experience a rear-end or transmission failure during the entire 1970 season.

All drive-line components were Ford's best and were required to handle the high-winding, canted-valve Trans-Am Boss 302 engine. The engines turned out 460 HP from one four-barrel carburetor and a 10.5:1 compression ratio. Stopping was just as good with 11.7-inch diameter disc brakes up front and 10.5-inch discs on the rear—a total of 374 square inches of swept area. Panic stops from 80 mph were well controlled, reaching 0 in 180 feet, despite the car's curb weight of 3240 pounds.

Wheels were 15 X 8-inch Minilites fitted with Firestone 11.50s on the front and 12.00s on the rear. Steering was just 2.2 turns lock-to-lock. With a final-drive ratio of 4.33:1, top speed was more than 150 mph at 7500 rpm, but drivers frequently took the engines to 9000 rpm in the heat of battle for around 175 mph. Bud Moore claimed his Boss 302s could pull 1.1g lateral acceleration, giving them tremendous cornering ability.

Moore's Mustangs went up against Roger Penske's Traco-powered, AMC sponsored Javelins driven by Mark Donohue and Pete Revson, Jim Hall's Chaparral Camaros, Dan Gurney's All American Racer Barracudas, Pete Hutchinson's Keith Black-powered Dodge Challengers, Jerry Titus' Firebirds and many other Trans-Am entries. But the Javelins were the only real competition as the Bud Moore Mustangs proved to be the team to beat.

After taking wins in the first four races, Moore had a huge lead in points, but the ever-present Penske Javelins pressed on. In the final analysis, though, they really never got close.

Moore's Boss 302 Mustangs took the Trans-Am championship in 1970, the third victory for Ford in five years of racing the series. But it was

Three Boss 302 team cars were campaigned during 1970 by Parnelli Jones and George Follmer who combined to win six Trans-Am races with five seconds. These 5-liter Mustangs were so successful that their end-of-season point total almost doubled Camaro and were more closely challenged by factory Javelins from the Roger Penske American Motors team trailing 59 to 72 points.

the last year for competing factory-sponsored teams. All but Penske's Javelins were gone for the '71 season. Trans-Am racing was left to independents and dashed SCCA's hopes for an even more popular season that year. Without factory teams, the Trans-Am series failed to draw the spectators it had achieved earlier and interest waned to an all-time low.

CHEVRON B19

Development of the earlier Chevron B8 brought the B16 sports car that later became the B19 Spyder late in the 1970 European 2-liter championship series. The B19 was essentially a B16 with an open body.

Chevron B19 Spyder was capable of putting the test to far more powerful cars simply because of its light weight and extremely good handling. Top speed of the Ford-Cosworth FVC 1800cc engine was not all that high, but being quick through the turns produced remarkably good lap times. Twisty tracks with short straights were what the B19 was bred for.

Following close on the heels of his great success, the B8, Derek Bennett introduced his magnificent B16 coupe as a step up in racing stakes. The B16 built upon the B8 and retained many of its qualities, ease of maintenance, durability and good value for the money, while its purpose was FIA's inaugural European 2-liter Sports Car Championship of 1970.

In terms of styling, the stunningly attractive B16 was a smashing success, a timeless beauty. Not only was it very appealing, it was also relatively inexpensive for a fully developed racing machine—around $13,000 complete with a Cosworth FVC four-cylinder and Hewland FT200 transaxle.

In its 1969 racing debut, Brian Redman wheeled the works B16 around the Eifel mountain circuit in the Nurburgring 500 Km. Aligned

against Redman and the first customer B16 were three works four-valve Abarths with 240 HP, various Porsches and an Alfa Romeo T33. Because the Cosworth FVC was not ready, the Chevrons ran a smaller 215-HP Cosworth FVA. Even so, Redman took the pole with a time of 6.4 seconds ahead of Herbert Schultze's Abarth. In a masterful display of driving, Redman pulled farther and farther away from the 83 car field to post an incredible margin of more than 2 minutes ahead of Schultze. The customer car was gridded 17th at the start and finished eighth to complete the Chevron entries and thus proved the overall soundness of the B16 design.

By March of 1970, 19 of the new Chevrons had been placed in customer hands. In advertisements, the B16s were said to be the ultimate in contemporary 2-liter sports racing-car design. No doubt they were as shown by John Burton winning the first British round of the 2-liter championship series at Snetterton.

But far greater acclaim for the cars was earned by Brian Redman when he took pole at Thruxton against top-rank cars. Before a huge television audience, Redman was initially outdragged by a Ferrari 512S, David Piper in a Lola T70 and Jo Siffert in a Porsche 917. But he hounded Siffert, his driving partner in the 917K Gulf-Porsches and earlier 908s, throughout the race to finish second, an excellent showing. Against the 4.5-liter, 630-HP Porsche that was capable of over 220 mph at LeMans, the little Chevron B16 with its top of 150 mph showed that superb handling in a featherweight car had a lot of potential.

Beautiful B16 coupe was Derek Bennett's styling masterpiece. These cars contested Group 6 Sports Car class races and were difficult to beat.

CHEVRON B19
1970

1800cc/110-CID DOHC Ford-Cosworth FVC in-line 4-cylinder
245 HP @ 8500 rpm
5-speed Hewland FT200 transaxle
1100 lb, fiberglass body w/tubular spaceframe
all independent coil-spring suspension

That lightweight formula was the theme of the B16's greatest adversary in 1970. Eric Broadley's open Lola T-210 was nearly 200-pounds lighter at just over 1000 pounds, and with a well-developed Cosworth FVC engine turning up 245 HP, Jo Bonnier was able to out-qualify the Chevrons almost every time.

Although the matchup seemed to favor the Lola, Redman's driving ability in the works Chevron balanced the equation. In the season opener on the new Paul Ricard circuit of southern France, he and Bonnier ran away from the field in their own race. When the Lola dropped out, Redman won, but it was clear that Chevron needed an improved car to compete against Lola.

Bennett began the B19, an open car similar to the Lola and 908/3 Porsches, as his answer to the lighter Lola. No one could have predicted that the outcome of the first International 2-liter Championship would have come down to this car and a last corner dice after 500 Km of racing.

The series was not dominated by a single marque, and along with the Chevrons and Lolas, there were Porsches, Abarths and Alfa Romeos that provided heated competition throughout the series.

The Type 907 Porsches ran 2-liter, flat eight-cylinder engines developed from Porsche's Grand Prix efforts of the early 1960s. However, these sophisticated engines proved to lack durability against the in-line four-cylinder Cosworth-powered cars, and the Type 906 and 910 became the top Porsches. Even though temperamental, 907s did take a second and a third place during the 2-liter season. (With 220 HP on tap in a 1430-pound car, Bill Bradley won the 1968 RAC British Sports Car Championship in Group 4 with a 906.)

Fiat-Abarth Sports 2000 cars with their twin-cam, four-valves-per-cylinder engines were a real threat to both Chevron and Lola, but lack of organization seemed to be the team's downfall. However, they scored a

1-2-3 sweep on Abarth's home turf at Mugello in Italy, and took two seconds and four thirds to finish a distant third in the championship. These five-speed Sports 2000 Abarths developed some 250 HP at 8000 rpm. At 1265 pounds, they were strikingly stylish and were capable cars lacking only refinement to be championship caliber.

Developed from the B16, the first Chevron B19 was mostly a B16 fitted with a new open aluminum body. Later-production models received fiberglass bodies of the same shape. Bonnier's Lola was in effect a works car as he was European agent for Lola and his car went through extensive development at the factory. However, his T-210 was prepared and entered through his own Ecurie Bonnier of Geneva, Switzerland.

The Lola's only failing was temperamental brakes, said to be the source of the loss to Redman's Chevron in the final race. Ten rounds were scheduled in the European 2-liter Championship series (only nine were run) and produced a lot of exciting action where club racers with comparable cars could go up against name drivers like Redman and Bonnier.

Chevron had three wins, two seconds and three thirds going into the last round while Lola had four wins, one second and no thirds for a slim one point lead. The championship was hard fought and lasted to the last turn of the last race, a 500 Km bout at Spa. Redman in the new works Chevron B19 Spyder won the pole from Bonnier and the two battled it out to the end. Multiple lead changes through close-fought turns created a classic race with Redman getting by Bonnier through Spa's La Source hairpin to take an incredible victory. Chevron won the first European 2-liter Championship by one point!

Redman went on to dominate South Africa's Springbok series in the B19 Spyder, with six wins, to secure another title. With the 1970 2-liter season a great Chevron year, Derek Bennett's small works was a proven builder of championship cars.

176

'60s, when cars were cars and racing went on everywhere. The dull 1970s were being brightened up by the return of truly interesting machines, those that were remembered wistfully and wished for again. For more than a decade, new cars were expensive slugs while these older machines were recalled for what they really were, the fired-up spirit of true performance.

Then along came Steve Earle and friends who saw some fun in their old cars and formed the Historic Motor Sport Association in California. Leguna Seca near Monterey became the site of HMSA vintage races and the weekend of the nearby Pebble Beach Concours was selected to combine the return of old racing cars with the showing of the world's most-elegant cars. It wasn't long before the Monterey Historic Races became a mecca for sports/racing participants and fans who thoroughly enjoyed the return of these exciting cars.

Automotive magazine editors found vintage races interesting and offered their readers something new. Organizers spotlighted particular marques on an annual basis and drew cars from around the world, many from museums where the cars had not been run for many years. Famous personalities were once again attracted to the cars and contributed their unique aspects to the new sport. In a short time, vintage races drew thousands of people.

California, long recognized as the American hotbed of new automotive ideas, had bred another success. In Europe, automotive traditions have always been better maintained than in America and vintage-car events have long been part of the norm. But in America, vintage racing was a new phenomenon.

It wasn't long until a Florida-based organization began an old racing-car movement at Sebring. Ford Heacock put together a rather easy-going first event that was so well received that the Southeast Vintage Racing Association was soon formed. SVRA calendars rapidly expanded to include Road Atlanta, Mid-Ohio, Watkins Glen and other events of a non-regional nature. Thus, SVRA became the Sportscar

A line up of '60s machines ranging from FIA world-championship endurance cars to SCCA production cars.

Vintage Racing Association with events attracting huge turnouts along with famous drivers, builders and other personalities.

Within a few years, groups in regions near a race track formed their own vintage races and now enjoy huge success from the same simple formula: Respect the cars, keep them on the track and have fun.

189

WHERE IT'S AT

Antique Auto Racing Assn.
Rt. 1, Box 172
Ixonia, WI 53036

Atlantic Coast Old Timer's
55 Hilliard Road
Old Bridge, NJ 08857

Chicago Historic Races
825 West Erie St.
Chicago, IL 60622

Chicago SCCA
520 Dundee Avenue
Barrington, IL 60010

Classic Sports Racing Group
110 "F" Hamilton Dr.
Novato, CA 94947

Dallas Grand Prix
12700 Preston Road, Suite 155
Dallas, TX 75230

Formula Junior Registry, Ltd.
1740 Midland Avenue
Highland Park, IL 60035

Grand Bahama Vintage Speed Week
120 Copeland Road
Atlanta, GA 30342

Historic Motor Sports Assn.
P.O. Box 30628
Santa Barbara, CA 93105

Historic Racing Group
28811 Gordon Hill Road
Valley Center, CA 92082

New York SCCA
77-37 Kew Forest Lane
Forest Hills, NY 11375

Pebble Beach Concours
P.O. Box 597
Pebble Beach, CA 93953

Rocky Mountain Vintage Racing
3800 South Clarkson
Inglewood, CO 80110

Sportscar Vintage Racing Assn.
P.O. Box 2955
Lakeland, FL 33803

Vintage Auto Racing Assn.
1052 Olancha Drive
Los Angeles, CA 90065

Vintage Auto Racing Assn. of Canada
RR #2
Brantford, Ontario
Canada N3T 5L5

Vintage Motorcar Racing
350 Liberty St.
San Francisco, CA 94114

Vintage Racing Club of British Columbia
Vancouver AMF
British Columbia
Canada V7B 1W1

Vintage Sports Car Club of America
P.O. Box 441
Lakeville, CT 06039

Vintage Sports Car Drivers Assn
P.O. Box C
15 West Burton Place
Chicago, IL 60610

Vintage Sports Car Racing, Inc.
12525 59th Avenue North
Plymouth, MN 55442

Williams Grove Old Timers
One Speedway Drive
Mechanicsburg, PA 17055

Walter Mitty Challenge
P.O. Box 2263
Roswell, GA 30077

INDEX

190